Anxiety After a Panic Attack

Understanding the Fear of the Fear Itself

Corwin Kirkland

First edition, 2026

Published by Corwin Kirkland

Contents

Chapter 1: What Really Happens During a Panic Attack

Sarah gripped the handle of the shopping cart. Knuckles white. The metal cool under her palm. She hadn't planned on grocery shopping today—had been putting it off for almost a week, actually—but they were out of coffee, and Saturday mornings just didn't feel right without it. So here she was, standing in the cereal aisle under buzzing fluorescent lights, and something was wrong.

Started as a prickle at the back of her neck.

Started as a prickle at the back of her neck.

Then it spread. A wave of heat flushing up from her chest, crawling across her skin like something alive. Her heart hammered against her ribs—not from exertion, but with this frantic, uneven rhythm that seemed to echo in her ears, her throat, the space behind her eyes.

She blinked, trying to focus on the brightly colored boxes surrounding her. Cheerios. Frosted Flakes. Those organic granola brands she always meant to try. They seemed to swim slightly, edges blurring. A dull ache bloomed behind her eyes. Her hands went clammy. Her throat tightened.

This wasn't just feeling anxious about the grocery list.

This felt exactly like—oh God—like she was having a heart attack. Or a stroke. The thought shot through her like ice water: *I'm dying. Right here. In the cereal aisle.* She hadn't felt this scared since she was seven years old, lost in the department store at Christmas, wandering through racks of winter coats looking for her mother.

"Everything okay, miss?"

The voice startled her. An older man with kind eyes and a canvas shopping bag stood beside her cart, concern etched across his weathered face.

Sarah tried to speak. Her throat felt constricted. A small, squeaky sound escaped—not words, just air. She shook her head, unable to articulate what was happening. It wasn't just fear. It was this physical sensation of being utterly overwhelmed, disconnected from reality. The fluorescent lights seemed too bright now. Painful, almost. The chatter of other shoppers—someone laughing near the deli counter, a child whining for cookies—unbearably loud, pressing in on her from all sides.

She needed air.

Needed to *move*.

She abandoned the cart mid-aisle—still half-full, a carton of eggs sitting there beside the coffee she'd actually come for—and pushed past bewildered customers toward the sliding doors. Her legs felt strange. Like they might give out. The automatic doors took forever to open. Then cool October air hit her face, and she made it to a bench before her knees buckled. Gasping. Trembling. Lightheaded. Convinced she was about to pass out or die or both.

The literature calls this a panic attack. Clinically, it's a sudden episode of intense fear that peaks within minutes, bringing with it a cascade of physical symptoms—palpitations, sweating, trembling, shortness of breath, chest pain, nausea, dizziness. The DSM lists them all out, neat and categorized.

What that meant for me, early in my career, was sitting across from people like Sarah—people who'd had one of these episodes and were now terrified it would happen again—and trying to explain that what felt like dying was actually their body doing exactly what it was designed to do. Just at the wrong time. In the wrong place. For the wrong reason.

And immediately, I'd watch their faces shift. This look that said: *You don't get it.*

Because here's what I learned fast—probably the hardest lesson of my training, honestly—telling someone "it's just a panic attack" doesn't help. At all. It's like telling someone who's drowning that the water is only four feet deep. Technically accurate. Completely useless.

I remember one of the first patients I worked with who'd had a panic attack. Graduate student. Brilliant. Could explain complex theoretical frameworks with ease. But when she tried to describe what had happened to her in the library stacks while researching her dissertation, she kept circling back to the same phrase: "It felt like I was dying."

Not "I thought I might be dying."

Not "I was afraid I was dying."

It felt like.

The sensations were so visceral, so convincing, that her rational mind—the part that knew, intellectually, that twenty-eight-year-olds don't typically have heart attacks while reaching for a book on postcolonial literature—couldn't override what her body was screaming at her.

That's the thing about panic attacks that makes them impossible to dismiss as "just anxiety." They don't feel theoretical. They feel like a five-alarm emergency. Your body is sending every possible signal that something is catastrophically wrong, and your brain—trying desperately to make sense of those signals—latches onto the most dramatic explanation it can find.

Heart attack.

Stroke.

Brain aneurysm.

Complete loss of control.

But here's what's actually happening, and it's both simpler and stranger than that: your body's ancient emergency broadcast system has been activated. Not because you're in danger. Because something—stress, a stray thought, a bodily sensation, even just the memory of the last time this happened—has been misinterpreted as a threat.

Now, I can already hear what you might be thinking: *If I know it's not dangerous, why can't I just tell myself that and make it stop?*

Believe me, I asked the same question. Still do, sometimes, when I'm in the thick of it myself.

Because—and I should probably tell you this part—I've had panic attacks. More than I can count at this point. The first one happened years before I specialized in treating them, which feels almost comically ironic now. Like a cardiologist having a heart condition. Except panic attacks aren't a condition, exactly. They're more like a feature of being human with an overprotective alarm system.

Let me tell you about my first one, because I think the clinical explanation only gets you so far if you haven't felt what we're talking about.

I was on a plane. Window seat. Somewhere over Kansas, I think, though honestly I couldn't tell you for sure because I spent most of that flight convinced I was going to die before we landed.

It started the way these things often do—with a completely ordinary sensation that my brain decided to interpret as catastrophic. A tightness in my chest. Not pain, exactly. Just...pressure. Like someone had placed a heavy hand there and was pressing down, slowly, steadily.

Now, I'd been sitting for two hours at that point. I'd been hunched over my laptop working on a presentation. My posture was terrible—shoulders rolled forward, neck craned, the whole disaster. The tightness was probably just muscle tension from the way I'd been sitting.

But my brain didn't think "bad posture."

My brain thought "pulmonary embolism."

Which is insane, right? I was in my thirties. Healthy. No risk factors. But there I was, at thirty thousand feet, absolutely convinced that a blood clot had traveled to my lungs and I was experiencing a medical emergency that would kill me before the plane could land.

My heart started racing. Not just beating fast—*racing*, like it was trying to escape my chest. I could feel it everywhere. In my throat. Behind my eyes. In my fingertips gripping the armrest hard enough that my knuckles went white.

My breathing got shallow and rapid. Which, of course, made the chest tightness worse. Which convinced me even more that something was catastrophically wrong. I started sweating—not a light sheen, but full-body, soaking-through-my-shirt sweating. The woman in the middle seat glanced at me and shifted slightly away.

I looked around the cabin. Everyone else seemed fine. Reading. Sleeping. Watching movies on those tiny screens. No one else was dying.

Just me.

I considered pressing the call button. Asking the flight attendant if there was a doctor on board. But what would I even say? "I think I'm having a pulmonary embolism but I have no actual evidence of this except that my chest feels tight and my brain has decided to panic?"

The thought of saying it out loud—of having to explain what I was feeling to a stranger while everyone around me listened—made everything worse. What if they thought I was crazy? What if I *was* crazy? What if this whole thing was in my head and I was making a scene for no reason?

But also: what if I was actually dying and I didn't say anything and I just...died? In seat 17A? Would they have to divert the plane? Would everyone remember this flight as the one where someone died?

So I sat there. Gripping that armrest. Sweating. Heart pounding. Breathing like I'd just sprinted up a flight of stairs. Absolutely terrified. Absolutely alone with it.

And then—and this is the part that felt almost crueler than the panic itself—it started to fade.

Ten minutes, maybe fifteen, and the sensations began to subside. Heart rate slowing. Breathing evening out. The tightness in my chest loosening, like someone had finally lifted their hand.

I wasn't dying.

I'd never been dying.

But the fear had been real. The sensations had been real. The absolute conviction that I was in mortal danger—that was real too. And sitting there in the aftermath, exhausted and confused and deeply embarrassed, drenched in sweat with my shirt sticking to my back, I had no idea what had just happened to me.

This is what I mean when I say you can't just explain panic attacks clinically and expect people to go "oh, okay, got it, no problem then." Because when you're in it—when your body is screaming at you that something is catastrophically wrong—your rational mind doesn't have much say in the matter.

The rational mind is like a courtroom lawyer trying to present evidence while someone's actively setting the building on fire. Technically, the lawyer might have excellent points. Hard to hear them over the alarm bells.

So what's actually going on? Why does the body do this?

Think back to our evolutionary history for a moment. Our ancestors didn't face anxieties about deadlines or social media or whether they'd remembered to send that email. Their threats were immediate and physical. Predators with teeth and claws. Rival groups competing for resources. Natural disasters. Infections that could kill you in days, if not hours.

Survival depended on being able to react *instantly* to danger. Not to think it through, weigh the options, consider various courses of action, maybe sleep on it and circle back in the morning.

To *react.*

Run or fight. Now. This second.

And that reaction is hardwired into every human body, tucked into the oldest parts of our brain—parts that were doing their job long before we developed language or abstract thought or the ability to worry about things that might happen three months from now.

When Sarah's brain perceived a threat—and yes, even though the grocery store objectively posed no danger, her brain registered something as threatening—it triggered what we often call the fight-or-flight response.

That's not a metaphor. It's not a figure of speech or a simplified way of talking about stress.

It's a specific physiological cascade that happens in your body, with measurable changes you could track if you hooked someone up to the right equipment.

Here's how it works, and this part matters because understanding the mechanism is the first step toward changing your relationship with it.

The amygdala—a small, almond-shaped structure deep in the brain—acts like an internal alarm system. It's constantly scanning for threats, processing sensory information faster than your conscious mind can even register. When it detects something it interprets as dangerous, it signals the hypothalamus, which then activates the sympathetic nervous system.

This is where things get interesting. And, for Sarah, incredibly unpleasant.

Adrenaline and noradrenaline flood your bloodstream, preparing your body for immediate action. Your heart rate increases—dramatically—to pump more oxygenated blood to your muscles. You need to run? Your legs need fuel. Now.

Your breathing becomes faster and shallower, maximizing oxygen intake. Or trying to, anyway. What actually happens is you start breathing so rapidly that you're not fully exhaling, which throws off the oxygen-carbon dioxide balance in your blood, which can make you feel lightheaded and disconnected—that weird, dreamlike sensation people describe as feeling "unreal."

Blood flow shifts *away* from non-essential functions. Digestion? Not important when you're trying not to get eaten. Hence the nausea some people experience, or that strange hollow feeling in the stomach, or the sudden urgent need to use the bathroom. (Your body, in its wisdom, wants to lighten the load. Make you faster. Sorry if that's more information than you wanted, but it's real.)

Blood flows *toward* your limbs instead. Arms and legs. Fighting and running muscles.

Your pupils dilate to improve vision. Better to spot the predator. Better to see the escape route.

Your muscles tense, coiled and ready. This is why people often feel jittery or shaky during and after a panic attack—your muscles have been primed for action, flooded with fuel, and then you don't actually use them for anything.

Your palms sweat. This one seems random until you realize that slightly damp hands have better grip. Better for climbing trees or holding weapons or grabbing onto something while you run.

Even your pain threshold increases temporarily, in case you need to push through an injury to survive.

It's a remarkable feat of biological engineering. A system designed and refined over millennia to keep us alive.

The problem—and this is where the whole thing falls apart in modern life—is that this system doesn't differentiate between a genuine life-threatening situation and something our brains *interpret* as threatening.

It can't tell the difference between a charging bear and a crowded grocery store that feels overwhelming.

Between a hostile tribe and a work presentation that's making you nervous.

Between a predator stalking you through tall grass and the escalating worry that you might have another panic attack.

The alarm doesn't have a "false alarm" setting. It just has "alarm."

For Sarah, the sensory overload of the grocery store—the lights, the noise, maybe the vague background stress of her to-do list, maybe something she can't even identify—triggered this response. Her amygdala interpreted something as a threat. The cascade began.

And every sensation she felt in the cereal aisle? Every single one was a feature of this system doing its job.

The sensation of having a heart attack wasn't an indication that something was wrong with her heart. It was simply the feeling of an increased heart rate and muscle tension in her chest.

The dizziness? Changes in blood flow and breathing patterns.

The feeling that she couldn't get enough air? Rapid, shallow breathing disrupting the oxygen-carbon dioxide balance.

That terrifying feeling of being disconnected from reality, what clinicians call derealization? Extremely common during panic. Thought to be related to the way blood flow changes in specific brain areas, combined with heightened arousal and altered breathing.

The tunnel vision, the muffled sounds, the sense that everything around her was somehow unreal?

All features. Not bugs.

It's all physical. All explainable. All normal, in the sense that this is what human bodies do when the alarm goes off.

And—this part matters more than almost anything else I'm going to tell you in this book—all temporary.

This entire process, from the initial alarm to the full cascade of sensations, feels incredibly urgent and overwhelming because it's *designed* to be. Think of it as an internal emergency broadcast system. You know those alerts that take over your phone screen, the ones that blare at full volume and can't be dismissed until you acknowledge them? The ones that jolt you awake at 3 AM when there's a flash flood warning two counties over?

That's what your body is doing during a panic attack.

It's grabbing your attention. Demanding you take action. Prioritizing survival above absolutely everything else—your meeting, your grocery shopping, your dignity, your rational understanding that you're not actually in danger.

The system works perfectly when there's an actual emergency. See a car speeding toward you while you're crossing the street? You need that instant jolt of adrenaline. That burst of speed. That narrowed focus. You need your body to stop thinking and start moving.

But—and this is the kicker—the system can also misfire. A smoke detector goes off when you burn toast. No fire. No danger. Just a sensitive alarm responding to the wrong trigger.

When this emergency system misfires in the cereal aisle, or on an airplane, or in a library, you're left with all the sensations of mortal danger and none of the actual threat.

Which brings us to the real problem. And I need you to hear this, because it's the piece that most people miss—the piece I missed for a long time, even after I started specializing in treating panic.

The panic attack itself? However terrifying? That's just the opening act.

Ten minutes of acute fear. Maybe fifteen. Horrible while it's happening, but temporary.

The real cost comes after.

Here's what nobody tells you. What I wish someone had told me before my first panic attack, and what I now make sure every single person I work with understands from day one.

The damage isn't in the panic. It's in what you do next.

Not in the ten minutes of acute fear. But in the days and weeks and months that follow, when your life starts to quietly reorganize itself around the fear of it happening again.

Let me show you what I mean.

Sarah sat on that bench outside the grocery store for another ten minutes. Maybe fifteen. The initial wave had subsided, leaving behind something almost worse: a bone-deep exhaustion and this pervasive sense of unease that settled over her like a heavy blanket.

She knew, logically, that she was okay. An older woman who worked customer service had come out to check on her, offered water, asked if she needed them to call anyone. Sarah had declined, embarrassed, mumbling something about low blood sugar. The woman had nodded sympathetically and gone back inside.

But knowing she was physically fine didn't erase the memory of those terrifying minutes in the cereal aisle.

Her hands were still shaking slightly.

Her chest felt tight, though not like before—more like a bruise now, a soreness from how hard her heart had been pounding.

She kept replaying it in her mind, trying to understand what had triggered it. Had she been too stressed lately? Was it something she ate? Not enough sleep? Too much coffee yesterday? (The irony of that, given why she'd come to the store in the first place, wasn't lost on her.)

But more than trying to identify the cause, what she kept circling back to was the fear. The absolute conviction, in those moments, that she was dying. That something was catastrophically wrong with her body.

And now, sitting here with her heartbeat slowly returning to normal, she hated the unpredictability of it all.

Hated that her own body could betray her like that. Without warning. Without reason.

The thought of going back into the store filled her with dread.

What if it happened again?

What if next time it was worse?

What if she actually *did* collapse, or lose control completely, or have some kind of public breakdown that someone would film and post online and—

She noticed she was doing it again. Her heart rate picking up. Breathing getting shallow. Just *thinking* about the possibility of another attack was enough to start the cycle.

She took a deliberate breath. Looked around. The parking lot. The cars. The ordinary Saturday morning shoppers loading groceries into their trunks.

Normal. Safe. Fine.

And yet.

She still needed coffee. That thought made her want to laugh or cry or both. She'd come here for one simple thing—one simple, ordinary errand—and now it felt like scaling a mountain to even consider walking back through those sliding doors.

What if the cereal aisle triggered it again? What if she made it to the coffee but then had another attack at checkout? What if people stared at her, recognized her as the woman who'd had a meltdown earlier?

Sarah didn't go back in that day.

She drove to a different grocery store across town—one she'd never been to before, where the panic attack hadn't happened—and hurried through her shopping, hyperaware of every sensation in her body, ready to bolt at the first sign of trouble.

She made it through without incident. Got her coffee. Got home. Told herself it was fine, everything was fine, she'd just been a little overwhelmed earlier but she was okay now.

But something had shifted.

Over the next week, she found herself avoiding that first grocery store entirely. Then she started avoiding other places that felt similar. Big, bright spaces with lots of people. The hardware store where she'd been planning to buy paint for the bedroom. The Target near her house where she usually grabbed household stuff. Even the coffee shop she used to go to on Sunday mornings felt threatening now—what if the panic came back there? What if she was in line, waiting to order, and suddenly couldn't breathe?

Within a month, her world had shrunk.

Not dramatically. Not in a way anyone else would necessarily notice. But she felt it. The slow constriction.

She started doing more of her shopping online. Ordering groceries for delivery. Picking quiet, less crowded times when she absolutely had to go somewhere in person—early morning weekdays, late evening after the rush.

She turned down an invitation to a concert. Too crowded. Too loud. What if she needed to leave quickly and couldn't get out?

She stopped going to the gym she'd been a member at for three years. Too many people. Too enclosed. What if she had a panic attack on the treadmill?

She told herself this was just temporary. Just until she felt more stable. Just until she figured out what had caused the panic attack in the first place so she could prevent it from happening again.

But here's what she didn't realize—what I didn't realize for a long time, even after I'd started working with people who had panic attacks—was that this pattern of avoidance wasn't protecting her.

It was making everything worse.

Every time she avoided a situation because she was afraid of having another panic attack, she was teaching her brain that those situations *were* dangerous. That the panic attack was a genuine threat she needed to escape from. That her body's alarm system had been right to go off.

And the more she reinforced that message, the more sensitive her alarm system became. The hair trigger got even more sensitive.

Think of it like this. Imagine you have a smoke detector in your kitchen. Sensitive one—goes off when you're cooking bacon, when you toast bread, when you use the broiler. Annoying, but you learn to live with it. You open a window, wave a dish towel at it, and it stops.

Now imagine that instead of doing that, you decide the kitchen is too dangerous to cook in anymore. The alarm went off, right? Must mean there's danger. So you stop using the stove. You stop using the oven. You start eating out or ordering takeout for every meal.

The smoke detector hasn't learned anything from this. It's still calibrated exactly the same way. But *you've* learned that the kitchen is dangerous. That cooking triggers the alarm. That the only way to stay safe is to avoid the kitchen entirely.

Eventually, you might start avoiding other rooms that are near the kitchen. Or other kitchens in general—friends' houses, cooking classes, that apartment you were thinking of renting but it has a galley kitchen and what if the alarm goes off there too?

The danger zone expands. Not because actual danger has spread, but because you're not testing whether the alarm is accurately detecting real fire or just responding to normal cooking smoke.

That's what happens with panic attacks.

When you avoid the grocery store, you don't learn that the grocery store is safe. You don't learn that the panic attack was a false alarm. You don't learn that even if you'd stayed in the cereal aisle, even if you'd felt every terrible sensation and done nothing but stand there and wait it out, you would have been fine.

The panic attack would have peaked and subsided on its own. Because that's what panic attacks do. They're self-limiting. The body can't maintain that level of activation indefinitely—it's physiologically impossible. The sympathetic nervous system eventually exhausts itself. The parasympathetic system kicks in. Things calm down.

But when you run—when you escape—you never learn that.

Instead, you learn that escape is the only option. That avoidance is the only way to feel safe.

And your world gets smaller and smaller.

I've worked with people who stopped driving on highways because they had a panic attack in traffic once. Who quit jobs they loved because they were afraid of panicking in a meeting. Who turned down promotions, canceled trips, broke off relationships—all in an attempt to avoid the situations they associated with panic.

One woman I worked with hadn't left her apartment in six months by the time she came to see me via video call. Started with a panic attack on the subway. Morning commute. Crowded train. She'd felt trapped, unable to escape, convinced she was going to pass out or scream or do something humiliating in front of hundreds of strangers.

She made it to the next stop and got off. Called in sick to work.

Then she stopped taking the subway. Started taking buses instead. Lasted about a week before she had another panic attack on a bus.

Then she stopped taking buses. Started taking taxis, which was expensive but felt safer—at least she could ask the driver to pull over if she needed to get out.

Then she had a panic attack in a taxi and stopped taking those too.

Started only walking places. Only going to places within a few blocks of her building.

Then walking more than a block from her building felt threatening. What if she had a panic attack and couldn't get home quickly enough?

Eventually, even the hallway outside her apartment felt dangerous. What if she ran into a neighbor? What if she had a panic attack in the hallway and someone saw her? What if they called an ambulance and she had to explain that nothing was medically wrong, she was just...what? Crazy?

She wasn't agoraphobic because she was weak or broken or fundamentally different from anyone else.

She was agoraphobic because she'd done exactly what her fear told her to do: avoid the situations that triggered panic.

And the panic, unopposed, unquestioned, had taken over her entire life.

This is the cost nobody talks about. Not the panic attack itself—that's temporary, however awful it feels in the moment—but the slow, insidious way your life can contract around the fear of another one.

The invitations you turn down.

The opportunities you don't take.

The places you stop going, the things you stop doing, the version of yourself you stop being because you're trying so hard not to feel that terror again.

The promotion you don't apply for because it would mean presenting to the executive team and what if you panic in front of them?

The vacation you cancel because what if you have a panic attack on the plane?

The relationship that never starts because dating feels too vulnerable, too unpredictable, too likely to trigger the anxiety that might spiral into panic?

And here's the most painful part, the thing I need you to really hear: it doesn't even work.

People who avoid situations associated with panic don't have fewer panic attacks.

Often, they have *more*.

Because the hypervigilance—the constant scanning for danger, the elevated baseline of anxiety, the way you're always on alert for the first sign that a panic attack might be coming—creates the exact conditions that make panic more likely.

You're not protecting yourself by avoiding.

You're priming the alarm. You're turning the sensitivity up. You're teaching your brain that the world is dangerous and you need to be on high alert at all times.

Which means you're more likely to interpret ordinary bodily sensations as threats. More likely to notice your heart rate increase slightly and think "oh no, here it comes again." More likely to have that thought trigger actual fear, which triggers actual physiological arousal, which feels like the beginning of a panic attack, which triggers more fear, which triggers more arousal, and now you're in the full spiral.

You created the very thing you were trying to avoid.

Let me tell you about Marco. Software engineer. Thirty-four. Healthy. Ran marathons for fun—like, actually enjoyed running twenty-six miles, which I'll never understand but I respect it.

Started having panic attacks after his mother was diagnosed with a serious illness. Cancer. The kind where the prognosis is uncertain and the treatment is brutal and you spend a lot of time in hospitals that smell like antiseptic and fear.

The first time it happened, he was at his favorite coffee shop near his office, working on a deadline. Normal Tuesday afternoon. Familiar place. Nothing threatening. He'd been there a hundred times.

Suddenly, he felt intensely hot. Like someone had cranked up the temperature in the room by twenty degrees. He looked around—was anyone else sweating? Taking off their jackets? No one seemed bothered.

Just him.

His heart began pounding in his chest—not just beating fast, but *pounding*, so hard he thought other people might be able to see it. Like in cartoons, when the character's chest literally bulges with each heartbeat. He could feel it in his throat, his ears, behind his eyes.

And then he had this distinct sensation of being unable to breathe. Like his lungs had stopped working or the air had gotten too thick to pull in. He tried to take a deep breath and couldn't—or felt like he couldn't, which amounted to the same thing in that moment.

He scanned the room for an obvious threat.

Someone looking at him strangely?

A loud noise he'd missed?

Smoke? Fire?

Nothing. Just people typing on laptops and ordering lattes and having quiet conversations.

He started to sweat profusely. His hands shook so badly he couldn't hold his phone to call for help. He was certain—absolutely certain—that he was having a heart attack. That he was going to die right there, slumped over his laptop, and someone would find him hours later when they came to close up the shop.

He managed to get outside. Sat on the curb. Called 911.

The paramedics came. Checked his vitals. Ran an EKG right there on the sidewalk. Everything normal. Heart healthy. Oxygen levels fine. Blood pressure slightly elevated but nothing alarming given that he'd just called an ambulance.

They suggested he might have had a panic attack.

He didn't believe them. Panic attacks were for people with anxiety disorders, people who worried about everything. He wasn't like that. He was calm. Logical. An engineer, for god's sake. He solved problems for a living.

So he went to the ER anyway. Better safe than sorry, right? What if the paramedics had missed something?

They ran more tests. Blood work. Another EKG. A chest X-ray.

All normal.

The ER doctor said the same thing: probably a panic attack.

"But I wasn't even anxious," Marco told me later, when he finally came to therapy months after that first incident. "I was just working. I wasn't stressed about the deadline. I wasn't thinking about my mom. I was literally just sitting there drinking coffee and coding."

Here's what Marco didn't realize: panic attacks don't always follow the script we expect.

You don't have to be consciously anxious. You don't have to be in the middle of a crisis or worrying about something specific. Sometimes the panic comes out of nowhere—what clinicians call "uncued" panic attacks—triggered by something so subtle you don't even register it consciously.

Maybe his body was carrying more stress than he realized from his mother's illness. Maybe his baseline arousal had been elevated for weeks without him noticing. Maybe he'd had a fleeting thought he didn't even register—something about mortality or loss or fear—and his amygdala caught it and sounded the alarm.

Or maybe it was something even more random. A shift in blood sugar. A slight change in breathing pattern. His brain misinterpreting a completely benign sensation as dangerous.

It doesn't matter, really. The why isn't as important as what happened next.

Marco started avoiding that coffee shop. Then avoiding coffee in general—what if the caffeine had triggered it? Then avoiding his office, which felt too similar to the coffee shop. Then working from home exclusively, which his boss allowed because he was a good employee and remote work was already common in his field.

Within two months, he'd had three more panic attacks. One at home, which shattered his sense that home was safe. One at the grocery store, which added another place to his avoid list. One while out for a run—his marathon training, the thing he loved—which was maybe the worst one because running had always been his stress relief, his meditation, his escape.

And then he stopped running. Stopped leaving the house except when absolutely necessary. Stopped seeing friends, stopped dating, stopped doing basically anything that involved being away from his apartment—his supposed safe zone—for more than an hour.

The panic attacks didn't stop. They got worse.

Because Marco, like Sarah, like the woman who couldn't leave her apartment, like me on that airplane not knowing what was happening to me, was doing the most natural, most understandable, most absolutely counterproductive thing you can do when you have a panic attack.

He was running from it.

So here's the framework I want you to walk away with. The model that changed everything for me, and that I've watched change things for hundreds of people I've worked with.

A panic attack is not the problem.

Read that again. I mean it.

A panic attack is your body's emergency broadcast system going off. Unpleasant? Absolutely. Terrifying? Often. Dangerous? No.

Not to your heart. Not to your brain. Not to any of your organs or systems.

You will not die from a panic attack. You will not lose control in the way you fear—you won't hurt anyone, you won't "go crazy," you won't be permanently damaged.

The panic will peak and subside on its own. Always. Every single time. Because the body cannot maintain that level of activation indefinitely—it's physiologically impossible.

The problem is what you do after.

Do you avoid the place where it happened? That teaches your brain the place is dangerous.

Do you hypervigilantly monitor your body for any sign it might happen again? That increases your baseline anxiety and makes panic more likely.

Do you try to control or suppress every uncomfortable sensation? That makes you more aware of those sensations and more afraid of them.

Do you organize your entire life around not having another panic attack? Congratulations—you've just made panic attacks the center of your world. Your brain gets the message: this is a massive threat that requires constant vigilance.

The solution—and I know this sounds counterintuitive, maybe even impossible right now—is to change your relationship with the sensations themselves.

Not to eliminate them. Not to prevent them from ever happening again.

But to learn, through direct experience, that they're not dangerous. That you can feel them without running. That the panic will crest and fall like a wave, whether you fight it or not. That the worst thing that happens during a panic attack is that you feel terrified for a few minutes and then it passes.

That's it.

No heart attack. No stroke. No loss of control. No public humiliation. No permanent damage.

Just fear. Just sensations. Just your body's alarm system misfiring and then resetting.

When you learn that—when you *know* it in your bones, not just intellectually but through lived experience—panic loses its power over you.

You might still have panic attacks. I still do, occasionally, when I'm under unusual stress or my sleep has been terrible or I'm sick and my body's doing weird things. They're not pleasant. But they're also not catastrophic. They're not something I organize my life around ng.

They're just...a thing my body does sometimes. Like sneezing. Annoying, but temporary.

That's the destination. That's where we're headed in this book.

But we need to walk before we run. And right now, if you're reading this because you've had a panic attack, or several, or you're in the thick of anxiety about having another one, I need you to start with something simple.

Something you can do right now, today, before you even turn the page to the next chapter.

Start tracking your panic attacks—not to prevent them, but to observe them.

Get a notebook. Or open a note on your phone. And the next time you have a panic attack—or even just elevated anxiety that feels like it might be heading that direction—write down:

- What time it started - Where you were - What physical sensations you noticed (be specific: racing heart, sweating, dizziness, whatever you felt) - What you did in response (did you leave? Call someone? Try to breathe slowly? Sit with it?) - How long it lasted

Don't analyze it yet. Don't try to figure out why it happened or what triggered it or how to prevent the next one.

Just observe. Just record.

Because right now, panic probably feels like this monolithic, uncontrollable force that descends on you without warning and could last forever.

But when you start tracking it, you'll notice something: it's not monolithic. Every panic attack has a beginning, a peak, and an end. Usually within ten to fifteen minutes, sometimes less.

Every panic attack involves specific physical sensations—and those sensations, however uncomfortable, are just sensations. They're data. They're your body doing something. Not evidence of danger.

And every panic attack ends. Every single one. Without you dying, without you losing control, without the catastrophic outcome you feared.

Start collecting that evidence. Not to fix anything yet. Not to make the panic go away.

Just to start seeing it clearly. To start understanding what we're actually dealing with.

Because once you see it clearly—once you understand that the real enemy isn't the panic attack itself, but the fear of the panic attack and the life you've built around avoiding it—that's when we can start taking your life back.

One situation at a time.

One sensation at a time.

One moment of staying when everything in you wants to run.

That's what the next chapter is about—understanding your body's signals so clearly that you can start to distinguish between "danger" and "alarm malfunction." So you can start to trust yourself again. So the grocery store can just be a grocery store, and a plane can just be a plane, and you can get on with the business of living without constantly bracing for disaster.

But first: the tracking. Start there. Notice what's actually happening, not what you fear might happen.

That's your job for today.

Started as a prickle at the back of her neck.

The initial prickle on Sarah's neck—a seemingly innocuous sensation—reveals how easily our nervous systems can shift into high alert, setting the stage for a cascade of physical responses.

Chapter 2: Your Body's Emergency Broadcast System

In 2008, swimmer Dara Torres stood on the starting blocks at the Beijing Olympics at age forty-one—ancient by swimming standards. Before the race, a reporter asked how she managed the pressure at her age. Torres said something that stuck with me: "My body knows how to do this. I just have to stay out of its way."

That's the paradox of panic. Your body knows exactly what it's doing. The racing heart, the shallow breathing, the dizziness—these aren't malfunctions. They're a finely-tuned emergency response system doing precisely what millions of years of evolution designed it to do. The problem isn't that the system is broken. The problem is that it's responding to the wrong threat.

I learned this the hard way on a Saturday morning at a farmer's market in Portland.

It wasn't painful at first. More like someone had set a textbook on my sternum—heavy, but not crushing. Then the air went strange. Not gone, just... insufficient. Each breath felt like I was trying to inflate my lungs through a coffee stirrer. My vision started to narrow at the edges, like someone was slowly dimming the lights on a stage.

I was holding a peach. A perfectly ordinary peach.

Around me, families laughed. A kid chased a dog past a vegetable stand. Someone was playing acoustic guitar near the flowers. Normal Saturday morning gravity. But I'd been ejected into some low-orbit panic dimension where the same physical laws no longer applied. I set the peach down with the kind of care you'd use handling nitroglycerin. My hands were trembling.

A woman nearby—fifties, kind eyes, holding a bag of tomatoes—asked if I needed help. I heard myself say "I'm fine" while my internal monologue screamed the opposite at maximum volume.

I made it to my car. Sat in the driver's seat with the windows down. Waited for my heart to remember how to beat like a heart instead of a jackhammer. Twenty minutes, maybe? Could've been five. Time gets elastic when your body's alarm system is shrieking.

Here's what I didn't understand then: my body wasn't failing me. It was protecting me from a threat that didn't exist.

The physiological response we call panic is—speaking purely mechanically—remarkable. Adrenaline floods your system within milliseconds. Your heart rate spikes to push oxygenated blood to major muscle groups. Your pupils dilate to take in more visual information. Blood vessels in your extremities constrict to minimize potential bleeding if you're injured. Your liver dumps glucose into your bloodstream for immediate energy. Your digestion shuts down because who needs to process lunch when a predator is charging?

All of this happens before conscious thought. Before you can even form the sentence "I'm scared," your body has already initiated a cascade of changes designed to maximize your chances of survival.

That's the system working correctly.

What that meant for me, standing there with a peach, was that my body had detected a threat and deployed the full emergency response... to a farmer's market. No predator. No physical danger. Just me, some produce, and an overprotective nervous system that had forgotten how to distinguish between a genuinely life-threatening situation and a crowded public space on a Saturday morning.

The disconnect is disorienting. Terrifying, even. Because the sensations are *real*. Your heart genuinely is racing. You genuinely can't catch your breath. The dizziness, the tingling in your fingers, the sense that something catastrophic is about to happen—all real, all happening in your actual physical body.

But the threat isn't.

And here's where most people—including me, for months—get stuck. You might be thinking: "If the threat isn't real, why does my body keep sounding the alarm? Doesn't that mean something is actually wrong?" It's a fair question. If your car alarm kept going off every time a leaf touched the windshield, you'd assume the alarm was broken, right?

But your body's alarm system isn't malfunctioning. It's *miscalibrated*. There's a difference. A broken alarm doesn't go off when it should. A miscalibrated alarm goes off too easily, in response to stimuli that don't warrant a full emergency response. Your nervous system has learned—through repeated panic episodes, through weeks or months of hypervigilance—to treat certain sensations or situations as dangerous when they're actually neutral.

The fix isn't to replace the alarm. It's to retrain it.

Let me tell you about David, because his story illustrates this recalibration process in a way that still catches me off guard.

David was an architect. Forty-six years old, successful by any measure—his firm had designed two museums and a concert hall that won awards I can't pronounce. He worked the way a lot of high-achievers work: relentlessly, meticulously, with the kind of perfectionism that produces beautiful buildings and chronic anxiety.

His first panic attack happened at his drafting table on a Tuesday afternoon. He was reviewing blueprints for a library renovation—something he'd done thousands of times before—when his chest tightened. Not pain exactly. Pressure. Like someone was slowly tightening a belt around his ribcage.

His heart started racing. Not the gentle increase you get from climbing stairs—the hard, irregular pounding that makes you acutely aware you have an organ in there, working, possibly failing. He couldn't get a full breath. Each inhale stopped halfway, blocked by something he couldn't name.

David drove himself to the emergency room. Walked in and said, "I think I'm having a heart attack."

They ran an EKG. Checked his troponin levels (a protein that elevates during cardiac events). Took his blood pressure, his temperature, his full medical history. The ER doctor—a woman with gray hair pulled back in a practical ponytail—came back with his results and said: "Your heart is fine. This was a panic attack."

She handed him a photocopied pamphlet about stress management. Told him to follow up with his primary care physician. Sent him home.

David felt relieved and insulted in equal measure. Relieved because he wasn't dying. Insulted because if this was "just anxiety," why did it feel like his body was actively trying to kill him?

Here's what the pamphlet didn't explain: David's body wasn't malfunctioning. It was responding—accurately and efficiently—to years of accumulated pressure. His nervous system, constantly braced for potential failure, had become hypervigilant. Like a security guard who's been on high alert for so long that he starts treating every customer entering the building as a potential threat.

The tightness in his chest wasn't cardiac. It was muscle tension—years of unconsciously bracing against the possibility of making a mistake, missing a deadline, delivering anything less than perfection. His body, preparing for a threat that existed only in his mind.

The racing heart? Adrenaline, surging through his system to prepare him for the "fight" against impossible standards. The shortness of breath? His respiratory system responding to perceived danger by shifting into a faster, shallower pattern—getting ready to run from something that wasn't there.

His body was doing exactly what it evolved to do. It was just doing it at the wrong time, in response to the wrong stimulus.

I wish I could say I understood this immediately after my farmer's market episode. I didn't. I spent weeks analyzing my symptoms, Googling combinations of "chest tightness" and "heart attack" and "sudden death," convincing myself that the ER had missed something, that there was an underlying condition waiting to ambush me.

I became hyperaware of my heartbeat. Started checking my pulse multiple times a day. Would lie in bed at night with my hand on my chest, counting beats, trying to detect irregularities. The irony—that this vigilance was itself triggering the very symptoms I feared—didn't occur to me until much later.

Here's what I wish someone had told me then, in language clear enough to penetrate the fog of anxiety:

Your body isn't the problem. Your *interpretation* of what your body is doing—that's the problem.

When your heart races during a panic attack, it's not signaling imminent cardiac arrest. It's doing what hearts do when adrenaline hits the bloodstream. When you can't catch your breath, you're not suffocating. You're breathing in a pattern that *feels* insufficient but is actually delivering plenty of oxygen to your lungs. When you feel dizzy, you're not about to pass out from some mysterious neurological event. You're experiencing the effect of slightly constricted blood vessels—a normal response to changes in carbon dioxide levels.

None of this is dangerous. All of it is deeply uncomfortable.

And that discomfort—that gap between "this feels catastrophic" and "this is actually harmless"—is where panic lives.

Think of it this way: your body is broadcasting emergency signals. Those signals are real—the increased heart rate, the changed breathing pattern, the muscle tension. But the message you're receiving isn't the one your body is sending. Your body is saying "elevated alert, prepare for action." You're hearing "you're dying." The signal is accurate. Your interpretation is not.

This distinction—between signal and interpretation—is the first piece of the framework that helped me stop treating every racing heartbeat like a medical crisis.

Let's talk about what's actually happening in your body when panic strikes, because understanding the mechanics strips away some of the mystery. And mystery, in this context, feeds fear.

Start with breathing. During panic, your breathing pattern changes—usually becomes faster and shallower. This isn't random. It's part of the emergency response. Your body, anticipating the need to fight or run, adjusts respiration to deliver oxygen quickly to your muscles.

But here's the thing about breathing: it's not just about oxygen. It's also about carbon dioxide.

When you breathe, you inhale oxygen and exhale carbon dioxide. CO_2 isn't just waste—it plays a role in regulating blood pH, the delicate balance between acidic and alkaline in your bloodstream. Your body works hard to maintain this balance within a very narrow range.

When your breathing speeds up and becomes shallower, you exhale more carbon dioxide than usual. Your blood CO_2 level drops. This might sound harmless—less waste product, right?—but the drop triggers a cascade of effects.

Lower CO_2 causes blood vessels to constrict. They narrow. This constriction is part of your body's preparation for potential injury—if you're cut, narrower vessels mean less blood loss. Efficient design for actual physical threats.

But when there's no injury, the constriction creates problems. Your brain, which is extremely sensitive to blood flow, notices the reduced supply. You feel lightheaded. Sometimes your vision blurs or you see spots. The sensation is real and alarming—but it's not dangerous. It's just your brain protesting the temporary reduction in blood flow.

Meanwhile, your heart is racing. Partly because adrenaline is telling it to pump harder, faster, get ready for action. Partly because it's trying to compensate for those constricted blood vessels—working harder to push blood through narrower spaces.

Your hands and feet start tingling. Maybe your lips. That's the constriction too, combined with slight changes in nerve sensitivity caused by the pH shift. Again: real sensation, harmless cause.

I want to pause here because this is where a lot of people—myself included—get tripped up. You might be thinking: "Okay, but what if my situation is different? What if I actually *do* have a heart condition and I'm dismissing real warning signs as panic?"

Fair concern. Here's the honest answer: if you've been to the ER, if you've had EKGs and blood work, if multiple medical professionals have told you your heart is healthy, then the chances that your racing heart during panic is a cardiac event are vanishingly small. Could you have a heart condition that's been missed? Theoretically, yes. Is it likely? No.

But the fear is hard to shake because the sensations are identical. A racing heart during panic *feels* exactly like a racing heart during a cardiac event—because in both cases, your heart is actually racing. The difference is the cause. One is adrenaline preparing you for action. The other is a blocked artery or electrical malfunction. Same symptom, wildly different underlying mechanism.

If you're still uncertain, get checked. Get a thorough cardiac workup. Rule out physical causes. But once you have—once a cardiologist has told you your heart is healthy—you have to trust that information more than you trust your panic. Otherwise you're teaching your nervous system that the medical clearance wasn't sufficient, that the threat is still real, that your body's alarm system is correct to keep firing.

You're recalibrating the alarm in the wrong direction.

All of these sensations—the dizziness, the racing heart, the tingling—are your body trying to protect you. The system isn't broken. It's just firing at the wrong target.

But here's the second piece of the framework, the part that took me months to understand: the sensations themselves aren't the real problem. The problem is what you do *in response* to them.

I'm going to tell you what happens if you don't learn to change your relationship with these sensations. Not to scare you, but because the cost of avoidance is higher than the cost of the panic itself.

Maria learned this the expensive way.

Maria was forty-two, taught eighth-grade English, had a daughter who played competitive soccer. Her first panic attack happened at home on a Thursday evening while she was grading essays. Unremarkable trigger. She felt her chest tighten, her heart start racing, and within minutes she was convinced she was having a heart attack.

Her husband drove her to urgent care. They ran tests. Everything came back normal. "Anxiety," they told her. She went home confused and shaken.

The second attack happened two weeks later at Target. She was in the cereal aisle—I remember this detail because she told me she can't walk past breakfast cereal now without feeling her pulse spike—when the sensations returned. Tightness, racing heart, dizziness. She abandoned her cart and left.

After that, she started avoiding Target. Then all grocery stores, because what if it happened again in public? She began ordering groceries online.

The third attack happened at her daughter's soccer game. Standing on the sidelines, chatting with another parent, when the familiar tightness started. She grabbed the fence to steady herself. Made an excuse and sat in her car until the game ended.

She stopped going to the games. Told her daughter she had too much work, too many papers to grade. Her daughter, thirteen and perceptive, stopped asking her to come.

Then the attacks started happening at school. Not during class, thankfully—she could usually feel them building and would excuse herself to the bathroom. But the anticipation, the constant monitoring of her body for early warning signs, became exhausting.

She started calling in sick more often. Used her sick days, then started taking unpaid leave. Her colleagues noticed. Her principal noticed. Maria, who had loved teaching, who lit up when talking about her students' progress, started dreading Monday mornings.

She quit drinking coffee because caffeine made her heart race and that felt too much like panic. Stopped exercising because the breathlessness from a run triggered the same fear. Avoided crowded places, unfamiliar restaurants, anywhere she might have an attack and not be able to escape easily.

Her world shrank.

By the time she came to therapy, she'd stopped going to her daughter's games, stopped socializing with friends, stopped doing anything that might elevate her heart rate or make her breathless. She was living in an increasingly small circle of "safe" activities—and even those didn't feel entirely safe.

The panic attacks themselves lasted, what, ten minutes? Fifteen at most? But the fear of them, and the avoidance that fear generated, had cost her months of her life. Her relationship with her daughter. Her joy in teaching. Her sense of herself as competent and capable.

That's the real cost. Not the sensations themselves, but what you sacrifice trying to avoid them.

And here's the cruelest part: avoidance makes it worse. Every time you avoid a situation because you're afraid of panic, you reinforce the message that the situation is dangerous. Your nervous system logs it: "Soccer game = threat. Grocery store = threat. Coffee = threat." The list of threats grows. The world that feels safe gets smaller.

I watched this happen in my own life too, in smaller ways. After the farmer's market incident, I stopped going to crowded places for a while. Told myself I was being prudent, giving my body time to "recover" (from what, exactly, I couldn't articulate). I skipped a concert I'd been looking forward to. Declined a dinner invitation because the restaurant was popular and I imagined it being too crowded, too loud, too many potential triggers.

Each avoidance felt like relief in the moment. And each one made the next avoidance easier. I was teaching my brain that these situations were genuinely dangerous, that my panic response was protecting me from real threats.

I was making the problem worse while believing I was solving it.

So what's the alternative?

It starts with a shift that sounds simple but is genuinely difficult: moving from fear to curiosity. From treating your body's signals as enemies to treating them as information.

Let me give you a concrete example from my own recovery.

About six months after the farmer's market incident, I was invited to give a presentation at a conference. Something I used to enjoy—I'm comfortable speaking in public, or I was before panic convinced me I wasn't. But standing backstage, waiting for my turn, I felt it starting. That familiar tightness in my chest. My heart picking up speed.

The old pattern would've been: panic about the panic. Rush to the bathroom. Maybe bail on the presentation entirely, claim sudden illness.

Instead—and I can't fully explain what made me choose differently that day—I got curious.

I stood there backstage and paid attention. Not to my catastrophic thoughts ("You're going to have a heart attack in front of three hundred people"), but to the actual sensations in my body.

My heart was racing. Okay. Where exactly did I feel that? In my chest, obviously, but was it centered or more to the left? Was it a steady fast rhythm or irregular? (Steady, as it turned out. Fast, but consistent.)

My breathing was shallow. What did that feel like, precisely? Was I actually unable to get air, or did it just *feel* insufficient? (The latter. I took a slow, deep breath to test. The air went in fine. My lungs worked.)

My hands were trembling slightly. I looked at them. Watched the small tremor. It wasn't violent shaking—just a fine vibration. Adrenaline, I thought. That's what adrenaline does.

I didn't try to make the sensations stop. I just... observed them. Like a scientist noting data. "Heart rate elevated. Breathing shallow. Hands trembling. Chest tight."

And then—this is the part that still surprises me—I walked onstage anyway.

The sensations didn't disappear. My heart kept racing through the first few minutes of the presentation. My hands still trembled when I clicked through slides. But something had shifted. The sensations were still there, but they'd lost their power to control me. They were uncomfortable background noise, not a five-alarm emergency.

About five minutes into the talk, I noticed my breathing had slowed down. My heart rate was still elevated—I was speaking to a large audience, some adrenaline made sense—but it had dropped from "sprinting from a bear" levels to "giving a presentation" levels.

By the end, the tightness in my chest had released entirely.

Nothing magical happened. I didn't use any special technique. I just stopped treating my body's emergency broadcast system like it was announcing the end of the world. I acknowledged the signals, noted what they actually felt like (versus what my catastrophic thoughts said they meant), and kept going.

That experience taught me something the pamphlet from the ER never did: you can feel panic and still function. The sensations don't have to stop before you can move forward. They're uncomfortable, yes. Distracting, absolutely. But not dangerous. And not disqualifying.

Let's get specific about what's happening when you shift from fear to curiosity, because this isn't just psychological fluff. It's neurological.

Your brain has an almond-shaped structure called the amygdala that acts as your threat detector. It's constantly scanning your environment and your internal state for signs of danger. When it detects a threat, it triggers the emergency response—the cascade of adrenaline and physiological changes we've been discussing.

The amygdala is fast and efficient, but not particularly smart. It can't distinguish between a real threat (an oncoming car) and a perceived one (the memory of a previous panic attack). It just sounds the alarm and lets the rest of your brain sort it out.

When you respond to panic sensations with fear—when you catastrophize, when you interpret a racing heart as a sign of imminent death—you're essentially confirming to your amygdala that its threat assessment was correct. Yes, you're telling it, this *is* dangerous. Sound the alarm louder. The sensations intensify. The cycle continues.

But when you respond with curiosity—when you observe the sensations without judgment, when you note what you're actually feeling versus what you fear it means—you send a different signal. You're telling your amygdala: false alarm. No threat here. Stand down.

This doesn't happen instantly. Your amygdala, having been trained by multiple panic episodes to treat these sensations as dangerous, won't immediately believe you. It's going to keep sounding the alarm for a while, just to be safe.

But with repetition, with consistent practice of observing rather than catastrophizing, the pattern starts to change. Your nervous system begins to recalibrate. The alarm gets quieter. The sensations, while still uncomfortable, lose their terror.

This is the third piece of the framework: repetition without reinforcement. You have to encounter the sensations repeatedly—and respond to them differently each time—before your nervous system learns they're not dangerous. One time standing backstage, getting curious instead of catastrophizing, isn't enough. It's a start. But the recalibration happens through dozens, maybe hundreds, of these moments where you choose observation over interpretation, where you note the signal without amplifying the fear.

I want to circle back to David, the architect, because his story doesn't end with that ER visit.

After his first panic attack, David became hypervigilant about his body. Started checking his pulse constantly. Would press two fingers to his wrist, count beats, try to detect any irregularity. Bought a heart rate monitor—one of those fitness trackers that displays your BPM in real time. Wore it constantly. Checked it dozens of times a day.

He thought he was being responsible. Monitoring his health. Catching potential problems early.

What he was actually doing was training his nervous system to treat his heartbeat as a constant source of danger. Every time he checked his pulse, he was sending the message: this matters, this might be wrong, pay attention. His amygdala, eager to help, ramped up its surveillance. Started flagging even minor variations in heart rate as potential threats.

The panic attacks increased. Became more frequent. Started happening in situations where he'd previously felt fine—at home, at work, while driving. His body, now primed to detect cardiac threat, was finding it everywhere.

Three months after the first attack, David was having them almost daily. He'd lost twelve pounds because his anxiety killed his appetite. He was sleeping four hours a night, waking repeatedly to check if his heart was still beating normally. His work suffered—he couldn't concentrate, kept making mistakes on projects he could normally complete in his sleep.

He went back to his doctor. "I know you said it's anxiety," he told her, "but something is genuinely wrong. It's gotten worse. I think I need to see a cardiologist."

She referred him. He saw a cardiologist. Wore a Holter monitor for forty-eight hours to record every heartbeat. Did a stress test—walking on a treadmill while they monitored his heart's response to exertion. The cardiologist reviewed everything and gave him the same answer the ER had given him months earlier: "Your heart is healthy. This is anxiety."

"But it feels like I'm dying," David said.

"I know it does," the cardiologist told him. "That's what panic disorder feels like. Your heart isn't the problem. Your nervous system's interpretation of your heart is the problem."

She recommended therapy. Specifically, a therapist who specialized in exposure-based treatment for panic. David, desperate and out of other options, made the appointment.

The therapy didn't start with relaxation exercises or breathing techniques. It started with a question: "What are you afraid will happen if you stop checking your pulse?"

David thought about it. "I'm afraid I won't notice if something goes wrong. That I'll miss the warning signs of a real problem."

"And if you miss those warning signs?"

"I'll have a heart attack. I'll die."

The therapist nodded. "Okay. So checking your pulse feels like it's keeping you alive. Every time you check and your heart is still beating, you feel relief. Safe for another few minutes."

"Yes," David said.

"But the relief doesn't last. You have to check again. And again. The anxiety comes back every time."

"Yes."

"That's because the checking is the problem. Every time you check, you're reinforcing the fear that your heart might fail. You're teaching your brain that your heartbeat is something to monitor, something dangerous, something that might go wrong at any moment. The checking makes you feel safer in the short term, but it makes the anxiety worse in the long term."

David didn't believe her. Not fully. But he was willing to try.

The homework was simple: stop checking his pulse. Remove the heart rate monitor. Don't press his fingers to his wrist. When he felt the urge to check, just sit with the discomfort.

The first day was hell. He lasted two hours before caving and checking. The second day he made it four hours. By the end of the week, he could go most of the day without checking—though the urge was still there, constant and insistent.

But something interesting happened. The panic attacks didn't increase. They actually decreased slightly. And the ones that did happen felt less intense, shorter.

After two weeks without the heart rate monitor, David realized he'd gone three days without a panic attack. Three days. The longest stretch since this whole thing started.

"Why is this working?" he asked his therapist.

"Because you're no longer telling your nervous system that your heart is dangerous. You're letting it recalibrate. Your amygdala is learning that it doesn't need to monitor every beat, that your heart can be trusted to do its job without constant surveillance."

David's recovery wasn't linear. He had setbacks—days where the anxiety spiked and he checked his pulse obsessively, convinced this time something was genuinely wrong. But over weeks, then months, the pattern shifted. His nervous system, no longer fed a constant stream of "your heart might fail" messaging, started to relax. The panic attacks became rare. Then stopped entirely.

The last time I spoke with him, David told me he couldn't remember the last time he'd checked his pulse. "I don't think about my heartbeat anymore," he said. "It just does its thing. I do mine."

Here's the framework in full, the three pieces that make your body's emergency broadcast system make sense:

One: Signal versus interpretation. Your body sends real signals during panic—elevated heart rate, changed breathing, muscle tension. Those signals are accurate. Your interpretation of what they mean is not. The signal says "elevated alert." You're hearing "imminent death." Learning to distinguish between the raw sensation and the catastrophic story you're telling about it is the first step.

Two: Response determines recalibration. How you respond to the signals determines whether your nervous system learns they're dangerous or neutral. Respond with fear, avoidance, checking behaviors—you reinforce the threat. Respond with curiosity, observation, continued action—you retrain the alarm. The sensations don't have to stop before you move forward. You can feel panic and still function.

Three: Repetition without reinforcement. Recalibration takes time and repeated exposure. You have to encounter the sensations dozens of times, responding differently each time, before your nervous system learns they're not dangerous. One instance of choosing curiosity over catastrophe isn't enough. It's the beginning of a pattern you'll build through consistent practice.

This framework won't make panic disappear immediately. It's not a quick fix. But it gives you a map for understanding what's happening in your body, and a set of principles for changing your relationship with it.

So what do you actually *do* with this information? What's the Monday-morning action step that moves you from understanding the framework to applying it?

Start here: the next time you feel your heart rate increase—whether it's full panic or just the early tremors of anxiety—pause. Don't try to make it stop. Don't reach for a reassurance behavior (checking your pulse, seeking medical confirmation, leaving the situation). Just pause and get curious.

Ask yourself: Where exactly do I feel this? What does the sensation actually feel like, stripped of the story I'm telling about it?

You're not trying to calm yourself down. You're not trying to make the sensation go away. You're gathering data. You're observing. You're treating your body's emergency broadcast like information rather than threat.

This sounds small. It is small. It's also the entire foundation of recalibration.

Do it once, and nothing changes. Do it thirty times, fifty times, a hundred times—and you start to notice that the sensations, while still uncomfortable, have lost some of their terror. They're just sensations. Adrenaline doing its thing. Your nervous system running its security protocol. Not a harbinger of death. Not a malfunction. Just your body's emergency broadcast system, firing at the wrong target.

And once you stop treating the broadcast as catastrophic, the system starts to learn that it doesn't need to keep broadcasting quite so loud.

The next chapter will teach you how to deliberately trigger these sensations in a controlled way—something called interoceptive exposure—so you can practice this observation skill without waiting for panic to strike on its own. But for now, this week, just practice pausing. Noticing. Getting curious instead of catastrophic.

Your body's emergency broadcast system isn't your enemy. It's just miscalibrated. And recalibration starts with observation.

Here's what makes observation so powerful: it changes your relationship to the sensations without requiring you to change the sensations themselves. Most anxiety advice tells you to breathe deeply, relax your muscles, think positive thoughts—all attempts to turn down the volume on the broadcast. And sometimes those things help. But they also reinforce a subtle message: that the broadcast is dangerous, that it needs to be stopped, that you're only safe when it's quiet.

Observation takes a different approach. It says: the broadcast can be loud, and I can still be okay. The sensations can be intense, and I can still be safe. My heart can race, and I don't have to race after explanations for why.

This is harder than it sounds, because your brain is *very* invested in the explanatory project. When your chest tightens, your brain wants to know *why*. Is it your heart? Your lungs? That weird pain you felt last month? The brain doesn't like uncertainty, especially not about the body. So it generates hypotheses. It runs searches. It catalogs past symptoms and cross-references them with catastrophic outcomes.

And here's the trap: the more you search for an explanation, the more evidence you find. Because when you're scanning your body for signs of danger, you *will* find sensations. Your body is never perfectly still, perfectly quiet, perfectly comfortable. There's always a twinge, a flutter, a moment of lightheadedness, a slight irregularity. In a calm state, you filter these out as background noise. In an anxious state, every single one gets flagged as potentially significant.

This is why people with health anxiety can spiral so quickly. It's not that they're imagining their symptoms. The symptoms are real. The tightness is real, the dizziness is real, the racing heart is real. What's happening is that their attention has turned into a magnifying glass, making every normal bodily fluctuation look enormous and ominous. And the act of checking—taking your pulse, monitoring your breathing, testing whether that pain is still there—actually intensifies the sensations, which then feels like confirmation that something is seriously wrong.

Observation breaks this cycle by stepping out of the investigative mode entirely. You're not trying to determine whether the sensation is dangerous. You're not trying to figure out what it means. You're just noting that it's there, the same way you might note that it's raining outside. It's information, not a verdict.

And when you practice this enough, something subtle begins to shift. The sensations stop feeling quite so urgent. Not because they've changed, but because your reaction to them has. When you're not adding the second layer of panic—the fear of the fear, the catastrophic interpretation, the desperate need to make it stop—the sensations often peak and then naturally subside. Because that's what sensations do. They rise, they crest, they fade. The broadcast doesn't stay on at full volume indefinitely. It pulses. It fluctuates. It responds to perceived threat, and when no actual threat materializes, it gradually powers down.

But you only discover this if you let the sensations run their course instead of interrupting them with panic or avoidance. And you only let them run their course if you trust, even a little bit, that they're not dangerous. Which is why observation isn't passive. It's an active practice of tolerance. Of building evidence, sensation by sensation, that intensity is not the same as danger.

This is especially important because one of the cruelest tricks of anxiety is that it punishes you for feeling better. You have a good day, a calm morning, a week without panic—and then the anxiety comes roaring back, often worse than before, and you think: *See? I knew it wasn't really gone. I knew I wasn't actually getting better.* And that thought itself becomes fuel for the next spiral.

But here's what's actually happening: your nervous system has been on high alert for so long that calm feels unfamiliar, even dangerous. When things quiet down, part of your brain interprets that quietness as a setup for ambush. So it fires a test signal. A little surge of adrenaline, a quick spike of panic, just to make sure the alarm system still works. And if you respond to that test signal as though it's a real threat, the system learns: *Oh, good. Still needed. Better stay on.*

Observation helps you pass the test differently. When the surge comes, you notice it. You name it: *This is a test signal. My nervous system is checking to make sure I'm still afraid.* And then you let it be there without reacting, which sends a different message back to the system: *Not needed right now. Stand down.*

This doesn't mean the signals will stop immediately. Recalibration takes time. But each time you observe without catastrophizing, you're training the system to be a little less reactive. You're teaching it that not every fast heartbeat requires a full emergency response. That tightness in your chest isn't always a prologue to disaster. That feeling lightheaded doesn't mean you're about to faint.

And gradually, the false alarms become less frequent. Not because you've eliminated anxiety, but because you've stopped reinforcing the idea that the sensations themselves are the threat. You've separated the signal from the interpretation. You've learned to hear the broadcast without believing every word it says.

Because here's the truth: your body is not trying to torture you. It's not broken. It's not failing. It's doing exactly what it was designed to do—protect you from danger. It's just firing that protection response in situations where no protection is needed. And the way you recalibrate an overly sensitive system isn't by fighting it, or suppressing it, or trying to convince yourself that nothing is wrong. It's by observing it clearly enough to see what it actually is: a signal. Not a sentence.

That's the paradox of panic. Your body knows exactly what it's doing.

Though Dara Torres's insight highlights the body's innate wisdom, understanding *how* this system gets triggered and amplified is critical to breaking free from the panic cycle.

Chapter 3: The Fear of Fear

I'll never forget the woman who told me she'd started setting her alarm for 3 a.m. every night. Not because she wanted to wake up at that hour—she dreaded it. But her first panic attack had hit at 3:17 a.m., jolting her awake with the sensation that her heart was trying to punch through her ribcage.

Not because she *wanted* to wake up at that hour—she dreaded it. But her first panic attack had hit at 3:17 a.m., jolting her awake with the sensation that her heart was trying to punch through her ribcage. Three weeks later, she was still waking up every night around that time, drenched in sweat, pulse racing, bracing for the attack that *might* be coming. So she figured: if she set an alarm for 3 a.m. and woke herself up *before* her body could do it, maybe she could somehow stay ahead of the panic. Control it. Outsmart it.

Of course, it didn't work. The panic didn't follow a schedule, and the alarm just guaranteed she was exhausted and on edge every single day. When she told me this—sitting in my office, hands wrapped around a coffee cup she hadn't taken a single sip from—I could see the dark circles under her eyes, the way her shoulders were hunched forward like she was trying to make herself smaller. She looked at me and said, "I know it sounds crazy. But at least when the alarm goes off, I'm *choosing* to wake up. At least I have that."

I got it. I understood exactly why she was doing it. Because once you've had a panic attack, your nervous system doesn't just file it away as "unpleasant experience, moving on." It catalogs every detail: the racing heart, the tunnel vision, the feeling that you might actually be dying or losing your mind. And then it starts scanning—constantly, relentlessly—for any sign that it might be happening again.

The literature calls this anticipatory anxiety, which sounds clinical and sort of manageable, like a weather forecast you can prepare for.

What it *felt* like for me, after my own first attack in a subway car during grad school, was being trapped in a horror movie where I knew the jump scare was coming but not when. I'd be sitting in class, heart rate normal, breathing fine, and suddenly I'd notice my palms were a little sweaty. Was that sweat from the overheated lecture hall, or was it the early tremor of panic building? The moment I noticed it, my heart would speed up—not because anything was wrong, but because I was terrified of *noticing* something wrong.

Which, of course, made my heart race faster.

Which confirmed my fear that panic was starting.

You see the problem.

This is the fear of fear, and it's one of the cruelest tricks your nervous system can play. The actual panic attack—the original event that was terrifying but finite, lasting maybe ten or fifteen minutes—gets stretched into a constant state of dread that can last for weeks. Months. Sometimes years. You're not just recovering from *one* panic attack. You're living in the long shadow it casts, waiting for the next one to strike, and that waiting becomes its own kind of torture.

The anticipation warps everything. You stop trusting your body. Every flutter, every irregularity, every sensation that would have passed unnoticed before now demands interpretation. *Is this it? Is this the start?* You become a vigilance machine, scanning internally for threat, and the irony is that this constant scanning—this hyper-focused monitoring of your heartbeat, your breathing, the tightness in your chest—creates the very sensations you're afraid of.

Your body can't tell the difference between scanning for danger and *being* in danger. So it responds accordingly. The heart picks up. The breath shallows. And now you have evidence that something *is* wrong, which justifies more scanning, which generates more symptoms, which deepens the fear. It's a closed loop, and every rotation tightens the coil. You're no longer afraid of panic. You're afraid of yourself—of what your own attention can trigger.

She eventually turned off the 3 a.m. alarm, but she kept her phone on the nightstand for months afterward—a reminder that the anticipation of panic can be louder than panic itself.

She eventually turned off the 3 a.m. alarm. Not because she stopped fearing panic, but because she learned something counterintuitive: the way out of fear isn't to run from the sensations that trigger it, but to turn toward them on purpose.

That shift—from avoidance to approach—is the hinge on which recovery turns. But it doesn't arrive as insight alone. It comes through experience, often accidental at first, when someone discovers that the thing they've been running from isn't actually dangerous. That the racing heart they've been trying to stop with deep breathing and distraction doesn't lead to collapse. That the weird sensation in their chest they've been Googling for three weeks straight is still just a sensation, no matter how much attention they give it.

The first time this happens, it's usually not because someone decided to be brave. It's because they ran out of options. They were stuck in a meeting, or on a plane, or at their child's school play, and the anxiety came anyway, and they couldn't leave. So they sat with it. They felt the heat rise in their chest, the tightness in their throat, the prickling along their arms. They waited for the catastrophe. And then—nothing. The sensations peaked, hovered, and slowly faded.

The thing they'd been certain would destroy them just... passed.

That moment is disorienting. It doesn't feel like relief at first. It feels like confusion. Because if the panic didn't mean what you thought it meant, then what have you been afraid of all this time?

A man I worked with described this exact sequence. He'd had a panic attack during a work presentation six months earlier and had avoided public speaking ever since. He'd turned down a promotion that required it. He'd rehearsed excuses for why he couldn't attend team meetings. But then his boss put him on the spot during a client call, and there was no graceful exit. He felt the familiar knot forming in his stomach, the heat crawling up his neck. He was certain he would freeze, that his mind would go blank, that everyone would see him fall apart. Instead, he kept talking. His voice shook a little. His hands were damp. But he finished his point. The client asked a follow-up question. He answered it. The call ended. No one mentioned anything unusual.

Afterward, he sat in his car for twenty minutes trying to make sense of what had just happened. He'd been so sure that speaking in front of people would trigger a full panic attack. He'd built his entire life around avoiding that scenario. And yet, when it happened, nothing collapsed. The fear had been enormous. The outcome had been... ordinary.

This is the strange arithmetic of anticipatory anxiety: the fear is always larger than the event. The mental rehearsal is worse than the real thing. Because in your mind, you're not just imagining the panic—you're imagining yourself unable to handle it, and everyone watching, and all the consequences cascading forward from that moment. You're catastrophizing in high definition. But when the moment actually arrives, you're not watching yourself from the outside. You're just in it, doing the next thing, and then the next. The narrative collapses into action. And action, even uncomfortable action, tends to be more manageable than imagination.

The problem is that one accidental exposure doesn't rewire the brain. The man in the car didn't suddenly become confident in meetings. He still felt the anticipatory dread before the next one. But something had shifted, even if he couldn't name it yet. He had a data point now. A piece of evidence that contradicted the story his anxiety had been telling him. And data points, when you collect enough of them, start to form a pattern.

This is how the fear of fear begins to loosen: not through understanding, but through repetition. Not by analyzing why you're afraid, but by proving to your nervous system, over and over, that the thing you're afraid of doesn't do what you think it does. Panic doesn't kill you. Anxiety doesn't make you lose your mind. A racing heart doesn't mean a heart attack. The sensations are uncomfortable, sometimes intensely so, but they're not dangerous. And once your body starts to learn that—really learn it, at a level deeper than thought—the anticipation begins to lose its grip.

But here's where it gets tricky. You can't teach your body this lesson by thinking about it. You can read every book on anxiety, memorize every fact about the autonomic nervous system, understand intellectually that panic is not life-threatening, and still feel your stomach drop when you wake up with a tight chest. Because fear doesn't live in the part of your brain that processes information. It lives in the part that reacts before you have time to think. And that part only learns through experience.

This is why reassurance doesn't work. Why telling yourself "it's just anxiety" in the middle of a panic attack feels hollow. Why

Googling your symptoms for the hundredth time doesn't actually make you feel safer, even when the articles all say the same thing. You already know the facts. What you don't have yet is the embodied knowledge—the deep, wordless certainty that comes from surviving the thing you were afraid of, again and again, until it stops registering as a threat.

A woman once told me she finally understood this after her fifth panic attack in a grocery store. The first four times, she'd abandoned her cart and fled. Each time, the relief was immediate but short-lived. She'd feel safe in her car, safe at home, but the next time she needed groceries, the dread would start building days in advance. She'd make lists of everything she needed so she could get in and out as quickly as possible. She'd go at off-peak hours. She'd rehearse her route through the store. And still, halfway down the cereal aisle, the panic would hit.

The fifth time, she was tired. Tired of running, tired of the shame, tired of arriving home with half the things she needed because she'd bolted before finishing. So when the panic started, she didn't leave. She stood there, gripping the handle of her cart, feeling her heart slam against her ribs. She thought she might pass out. She thought people were staring. She thought she was going to have to call someone to come get her. But she didn't do any of those things. She just stood there. And the panic, after a few minutes that felt like hours, began to recede. Not all at once. Not cleanly. But it faded. And she was still standing.

She didn't finish her shopping that day. But she didn't run, either. And the next time she went to the store, the panic came again, but it was a little less intense. A little shorter. By the tenth visit, she could feel the anxiety rising and think, "Okay, here it is again," without the added layer of terror about the terror. The panic itself hadn't become pleasant. But it had become predictable. Manageable. Boring, even.

That's the shift. Panic stops being an emergency and starts being an inconvenience. The fear of fear dissolves when fear itself becomes familiar.

But getting to that point requires something most people instinctively resist: deliberately putting yourself in the situations that trigger your anxiety. This is the foundation of exposure therapy, and it's brutally counterintuitive. Every instinct in your body is screaming at you to avoid the thing that makes you feel this way. Your brain has categorized certain situations—crowds, enclosed spaces, being far from home, whatever your particular triggers are—as dangerous. And now someone is suggesting you walk directly toward them?

It sounds absurd. It sounds like torture. And yet, it's the most effective intervention we have for breaking the cycle of anticipatory anxiety.

Here's why it works: avoidance teaches your brain that the thing you're avoiding is genuinely dangerous. Every time you flee a situation because you're afraid of panicking, you confirm to your nervous system that panic is something worth fleeing. You never get the chance to learn that you could have stayed, that the panic would have passed, that nothing terrible would have happened. So the next time the situation comes up, your fear response is even stronger, because the last data point your brain logged was: "We ran, and that kept us safe."

But exposure flips the script. When you stay in the situation despite the fear, you generate a new data point: "I felt panic, I stayed, and I survived." Do that enough times, and your brain starts to recalibrate. The situation gets reclassified. Not as safe, necessarily, but as not-dangerous. The alarm system stops blaring quite so loudly. The anticipatory dread before the situation starts to fade, because your brain no longer has evidence that this is a scenario requiring emergency protocols.

This doesn't happen overnight. And it doesn't happen by white-knuckling your way through situations while silently freaking out. Effective exposure requires a specific approach: you go into the situation voluntarily, you stay until the anxiety starts to come down on its own (not because you distracted yourself or used a safety behavior, but because it naturally peaked and subsided), and you do it repeatedly, with enough frequency that your brain has a chance to update its threat assessment.

The key is that you're not trying to eliminate the anxiety. You're trying to change your relationship to it. You're proving to yourself that you can feel anxious and still function. That anxiety is uncomfortable but not unbearable. That you don't need to control it or fix it or make it go away in order to do the things that matter to you.

A younger man I worked with had developed a fear of driving after a panic attack on the highway. He'd been on his way to visit family, stuck in slow-moving traffic, when the panic hit. He'd managed to pull over and call a friend to pick him up, leaving his car on the shoulder. For months afterward, he avoided highways entirely. Then he started avoiding any drive longer than ten minutes. Eventually, he was taking rideshares to work, even though he owned a car.

When we started exposure work, we didn't begin with the highway. We started with him sitting in his parked car in his driveway. Just sitting there, engine off, feeling whatever came up. The first time, he lasted three minutes before the claustrophobia became unbearable and he got out. The second time, five minutes. By the tenth session, he could sit in the car for twenty minutes, feeling anxious but not panicked, and then go back inside without it ruining his day.

From there, we built up gradually: engine on, still parked. Short drives around his neighborhood. Slightly longer drives on side streets. Each step involved sitting with the discomfort, noticing the anticipatory dread before the drive and the relief after, and recognizing that the actual driving was never as catastrophic as the anticipation suggested.

It took him three months to get back on the highway. And even then, his first highway drive was five minutes, one exit, with a friend in the passenger seat. But he did it. And he did it again the next week. And the week after that. The anxiety didn't vanish. But it stopped dictating his choices.

This is what people miss when they think about exposure: it's not about becoming fearless. It's about becoming less controlled by fear. The goal isn't to never feel anxious again. The goal is to feel anxious and keep moving forward anyway, until your brain learns that forward movement is possible even in the presence of fear.

But there's a crucial nuance here, one that separates effective exposure from retraumatization. You have to approach the feared situation with a degree of willingness, not force. If you're white-knuckling through it, gritting your teeth and enduring it while every fiber of your being is screaming to escape, you're not teaching your brain that the situation is safe. You're just teaching it that you can survive misery. That's not the same thing.

Effective exposure requires what acceptance-based therapies call "willingness"—a kind of openness to the experience, even if the experience is uncomfortable. It's the difference between clenching your fist around a hot coal and opening your hand to let it pass through. Both involve contact with the discomfort, but one creates more suffering than the other.

This is where mindfulness intersects with exposure. When you're in a situation that triggers anxiety, the instinct is to brace against it—to tense up, hold your breath, mentally fight the sensations. But that bracing is itself a form of resistance, and resistance amplifies discomfort. What helps is the opposite: softening into the sensations, getting curious about them, describing them to yourself without judgment. "There's tightness in my chest. My palms are sweating. My thoughts are racing." Not, "Oh God, here it comes, this is going to be awful, I can't handle this," but simply, "This is what anxiety feels like right now."

It sounds simplistic. It sounds like the kind of thing someone who's never had a panic attack would suggest. But it's not about making the anxiety pleasant. It's about making it less sticky. When you describe a sensation without adding a layer of catastrophic interpretation, it becomes just a sensation. Uncomfortable, yes, but not dangerous. And sensations, when you stop feeding them with frightened attention, tend to shift and change on their own.

A woman told me she practiced this while sitting in her dentist's waiting room, a place that had become loaded with panic after a particularly rough cleaning during which she'd had an attack. She'd been avoiding the dentist for two years, which was starting to have real consequences for her health. So she made an appointment, and then she made herself show up.

Sitting in the waiting room, she felt the anxiety building. Her instinct was to run. Instead, she started narrating her experience to herself, silently, like a sports commentator. "Okay, heart rate's picking up. There's that familiar tightness. Hands are cold. Thoughts are saying this is a mistake, I should leave. But I'm still sitting here. The chair is solid. My feet are on the floor. I'm breathing." Not fighting any of it. Just observing. And slowly, incrementally, the panic began to lose its edge. Not because she'd done anything to fix it, but because she'd stopped resisting it.

She still felt anxious when the hygienist called her name. She felt anxious in the chair. But she made it through the appointment. And two weeks later, when she had to go back for a follow-up, the anticipatory dread was noticeably smaller. Not gone. Smaller.

This is the unglamorous truth about recovering from anticipatory anxiety: it happens in tiny increments, through repeated exposure to the thing you've been avoiding, and it requires a willingness to feel uncomfortable without needing to escape. There's no shortcut. No hack. No app that will do it for you. Just the slow, unspectacular work of teaching your nervous system that the world is safer than it thinks.

And here's the part that no one tells you at the beginning: as you start to do this work, as you begin exposing yourself to feared situations and staying present with the discomfort, the anxiety often gets worse before it gets better. Because you're no longer avoiding. You're no longer running. So you're actually feeling the full intensity of the fear you've been dodging. And that can be destabilizing, especially if you thought that "doing the work" meant you'd start feeling better immediately.

But that initial spike is actually a good sign. It means you're engaging with the fear instead of avoiding it. It means you're generating new experiences, new data points. And those data points, over time, are what change the brain's threat assessment. The process is uncomfortable, but it's not dangerous. And gradually, the anticipation begins to shrink.

Because here's what happens when you stop avoiding: the situations you've been afraid of start to lose their power. The grocery store becomes just a grocery store again. The highway becomes just a route. Your own heartbeat becomes just a physical sensation, not a harbinger of doom. And the fear of fear, which has been running the show for so long, begins to quiet.

It doesn't disappear entirely. Most people who recover from panic disorder will tell you that they still feel anxious sometimes, that they still notice their heart rate spiking or their breath quickening in certain situations. But they're no longer afraid of those sensations. They've learned, through direct experience, that a racing heart is just a racing heart. That anxiety is just anxiety. Uncomfortable, yes. Worthy of attention, maybe. But not an emergency. Not anymore.

The woman who set her alarm for 3:17 AM wasn't just afraid of having another attack; she was trapped in a self-fulfilling prophecy, prompting us to consider how anticipation shapes our experience of anxiety.

Chapter 4: Interoceptive Exposure

Think about the last time you were truly startled—not by anything dangerous, just genuinely caught off guard. A door slamming in the wind. Someone walking up behind you when you thought you were alone. What happened in your body in that first half-second before your brain caught up?

That fleeting moment between startle and rationalization is precisely what interoceptive exposure aims to recapture—a space where sensation isn't immediately labeled as threatening, trusting that your body, even in its heightened state, *knows* what it's doing.

Your heart jumped. Maybe skipped a beat entirely. Heat rushed up your neck. Your chest tightened. For a moment—just a flash—you couldn't quite catch your breath.

Then your rational mind kicked in. *Just the wind. Just a friend. Nothing to worry about.* And within seconds, your body settled. The whole thing passed so quickly you probably didn't give it another thought.

Now imagine that same sequence of sensations—the racing heart, the tight chest, the breathlessness—but this time, there's no door, no person, no external cause. Just your body, doing its thing. And instead of your rational mind saying *nothing to worry about,* it says: *Oh god, it's happening again.*

That's the trap.

After a panic attack, those completely normal bodily sensations get flagged. Marked as dangerous. Your nervous system starts treating a slightly elevated heart rate like a warning siren. And the more you try to avoid those sensations, the louder that siren gets. The more you check for them, monitor them, brace against them, the more your brain learns that they *must* be dangerous.

The clinical term for this is interoceptive conditioning—your amygdala, the brain's threat-detection center, learns to associate certain internal sensations with mortal danger. It doesn't care about logic. It cares about patterns. And the pattern it's learned is: *racing heart equals panic attack equals catastrophe.*

What that meant for me was that I became terrified of my own body.

I'd be sitting at my desk, perfectly calm, and I'd notice my heart rate pick up just slightly. Maybe I'd shifted position. Maybe I'd had too much coffee. Didn't matter. The moment I noticed it, my entire system went on high alert. *Is this it? Is this the start?* And of course, the moment I started monitoring my heart rate with that kind of intensity, it *did* pick up. Because anxiety raises your heart rate. Which gave me more to be anxious about. Which raised it further.

I was creating the very thing I feared.

Here's what nobody tells you about avoidance: it works. In the short term, it works beautifully. You feel your heart start to race, you sit down, you take deep breaths, you distract yourself—and the sensation passes. Relief floods in. You've "prevented" the panic attack. Your nervous system logs this as: *Avoidance saved me. Avoidance works. I must avoid these sensations at all costs.*

But here's what's actually happening. Every time you avoid a sensation, you're teaching your brain that the sensation *was* dangerous. You're confirming the false alarm. And your brain gets better and better at detecting these "threats." The threshold gets lower. The alarm gets louder. The window of tolerance gets narrower.

Six months after my first panic attack, I was afraid to exercise. I was afraid to drink coffee. I was afraid to watch intense movies or have difficult conversations or do anything that might elevate my heart rate. I was afraid to feel my own aliveness.

That's the cost. Not just the panic attacks themselves, but the slow, insidious narrowing of your life. The things you stop doing. The experiences you opt out of. The way you start organizing your entire existence around avoiding certain sensations in your body.

You become smaller. Quieter. More careful.

You trade spontaneity for control, possibility for predictability. And the cruelest part? It doesn't even work. Because you can't control your body that completely. You can't prevent your heart from ever racing, your breath from ever catching, your hands from ever trembling. These are autonomous processes. And when they do happen—when you're sitting in a meeting or standing in line at the grocery store and your heart decides to pick up speed for no reason you can identify—the panic that follows is even worse. Because now you've failed. You've lost control of the one thing you were trying so desperately to control.

So what's the alternative?

Interoceptive exposure—the deliberate, controlled practice of evoking the very physical sensations you've been running from—is one of the most effective interventions we have for breaking this cycle. But understanding why it works requires letting go of the idea that the goal is to make these sensations disappear.

They're not going to disappear.

Your heart is going to race sometimes. You're going to feel dizzy sometimes. Your breath is going to catch sometimes. That's what bodies do. The goal isn't to eliminate these experiences. The goal is to change your relationship to them. To stop treating a racing heart like evidence of impending catastrophe and start seeing it for what it is: just a racing heart.

Let me show you what this looks like in practice.

I worked with a woman named Rachel—and I'm using her real name here with permission, because she wanted her story told—who developed a debilitating fear of breathlessness after choking on a piece of food at a restaurant. She hadn't actually been in serious danger; someone performed the Heimlich maneuver, the food dislodged, and within seconds she was fine. But her nervous system didn't care about the outcome. It cared about those terrifying seconds when she couldn't breathe.

Within weeks, Rachel became hyperaware of any sensation related to her breathing. A slight tightness in her throat. A feeling of not getting quite enough air. The sensation of swallowing "wrong." Each of these would trigger panic.

She started avoiding certain foods—anything that required a lot of chewing, anything that might "go down the wrong way." She stopped eating in public. Eventually, she stopped eating solid food altogether, subsisting mostly on smoothies and soup.

When she came to see me, she was convinced there was something physically wrong with her throat. She'd seen multiple doctors, had scans done, been checked for allergies and structural abnormalities. Everything came back normal.

"But I *feel* it," she kept saying. "I can feel that something's wrong."

And she could. She absolutely could. Because when you're that focused on a particular body part, scanning it constantly for signs of trouble, you *will* notice sensations. The question wasn't whether she was feeling something—she was. The question was what those sensations meant.

We started with something absurdly simple: I asked her to hold her breath.

She looked at me like I'd suggested she jump off a building.

"Just for five seconds," I said. "I'll time it. You hold your breath, you notice what you feel, and then you breathe normally again."

"What if I can't breathe again?" The question came out in a whisper.

"Then we'll deal with it. But I'm sitting right here, and I've done this exercise with dozens of people, and every single one of them has been able to breathe again."

It took her three tries to actually do it. The first two times, she started to hold her breath, felt the immediate urge to inhale, and gave in within a second. But on the third try, she made it to five seconds. Then exhaled. Then sat there, eyes wide.

"What did you notice?" I asked.

"I... I wanted to breathe. Like, really wanted to. My chest felt tight. I felt kind of panicky."

"And did you breathe again?"

She blinked. "Yeah."

"Okay. Let's do it again. This time, seven seconds."

We worked up gradually. Five seconds became seven became ten. Each time, she experienced that urge to breathe—that air hunger, that sensation of her body demanding oxygen—and each time, she breathed again. No catastrophe. No choking. Just temporary discomfort followed by relief.

The point wasn't to prove she *could* hold her breath. The point was to show her nervous system that the sensation of breathlessness—even deliberately induced—wasn't dangerous. That she could feel that discomfort and survive it.

From there, we added other exercises. Breathing through a thin straw for thirty seconds to create a sensation of restricted airflow. Taking rapid, shallow breaths to induce that feeling of not getting enough air. Each exercise was designed to evoke a mild version of what she feared, in a context where she had complete control.

And here's what happened: nothing.

Nothing catastrophic, anyway. She felt uncomfortable. She felt anxious. Her heart raced. Her palms got sweaty. She wanted to stop. But she didn't choke. She didn't suffocate. The sensations peaked and then—crucially—subsided on their own, even when she didn't actively try to make them go away.

This is the mechanism interoceptive exposure works on. It's not distraction. It's not positive thinking. It's habituation. Your nervous system learns, through repeated experience, that these sensations aren't dangerous. The alarm gets quieter. The threshold rises. The window of tolerance expands.

Rachel didn't do one breath-holding exercise and suddenly feel fine about eating solid food again. She practiced daily for weeks. Some days were easier than others. Some days the anxiety felt overwhelming and she wanted to quit. But she kept showing up.

Three months in, she ate a sandwich in my office. Her hands shook. She took tiny bites. She had to pause several times to breathe and remind herself she was okay. But she did it.

And when she finished, she cried—not from fear, but from something closer to grief. Grief for all the meals she'd missed, all the time she'd lost to this fear, all the smallness she'd accepted as normal.

Now let me give you the other side of this. Because interoceptive exposure isn't just for people with specific fears like Rachel's breathlessness. It's for anyone whose relationship to their body has become defined by vigilance and control.

After my own panic attacks, I became obsessed with my heart rate. I checked my pulse constantly—at my desk, in the car, in bed before falling asleep. I downloaded apps that could measure it through my phone's camera. I wore a fitness tracker that buzzed every time my heart rate exceeded a certain threshold.

I was convinced that if I could just monitor it closely enough, I could prevent it from spiraling out of control.

All that monitoring? It made everything worse. Because I was essentially teaching my nervous system that my heart rate was something to be afraid of. Something that required constant surveillance. And the more I watched it, the more it fluctuated—because anxiety itself raises your heart rate, which creates more anxiety, which raises it further.

So I started doing something that felt completely counterintuitive: I deliberately made my heart race.

I'd do jumping jacks in my living room. Thirty seconds, enough to get my heart pounding. Then I'd sit down and—this was the hard part—I'd just notice it. Not try to calm it down. Not take deep breaths. Not distract myself. Just sit there and feel my heart beating hard and fast in my chest.

The first time I did this, I lasted maybe ten seconds before I gave in and started doing breathing exercises to bring it down. The second time, I made it twenty seconds. By the fifth or sixth time, I could sit with an elevated heart rate for several minutes without needing to "fix" it.

And somewhere in that process, something shifted.

I realized my heart rate going up wasn't the problem. The problem was my interpretation of it. The story I was telling myself about what it meant. When I went for a run, my heart rate went up, and I called that "exercise." When I got excited about something, my heart rate went up, and I called that "enthusiasm." But when my heart rate went up for no reason I could identify—or worse, when it went up *because* I was anxious—I called that "danger."

Same sensation. Different story.

Interoceptive exposure gave me a way to rewrite that story. Not through logic or affirmations, but through direct, embodied experience. My heart can race, and I can be okay. My breath can catch, and I can be okay. I can feel dizzy or lightheaded or shaky, and I can be okay.

Not comfortable, necessarily. Not pleasant. But okay. Safe. Alive.

Here's what a basic interoceptive exposure practice might look like for you. Start with whatever sensation you fear most—elevated heart rate, breathlessness, dizziness, lightheadedness, the feeling of losing control. Pick one. Then find a simple, safe way to evoke that sensation deliberately.

For heart rate: jumping jacks, running in place, stair climbing. Start with thirty seconds. Notice what you feel. Where in your body do you feel your heart beating? How would you describe the sensation? Sharp? Fluttery? Pounding? Don't judge it. Don't try to change it. Just observe it.

For breathlessness: hold your breath for a count of ten. Or breathe through a straw for thirty seconds. Or take quick, shallow breaths for fifteen seconds. The goal is to create a mild sensation of air hunger or restriction, then observe it without intervening.

For dizziness: spin slowly in a desk chair for ten rotations, then stop and sit still. Notice the swirling sensation. Where do you feel it? Does it move? Change? Intensify? Fade?

For lightheadedness: stand up quickly from a seated position. Or hyperventilate gently for twenty seconds. (Be careful with this one—sit down before you start, and don't push it past mild discomfort.)

Do these exercises when you're relatively calm, not in the middle of a panic attack. Start small. If thirty seconds feels like too much, do fifteen. If fifteen feels like too much, do five. The point isn't to overwhelm yourself. The point is to gradually expand your tolerance for discomfort.

And here's the crucial part: after you induce the sensation, resist the urge to immediately "fix" it.

Sit with it. Let it be there. Notice it rise, peak, and—this is what your nervous system needs to learn—subside on its own. Because it will. Every sensation you're afraid of is temporary. Every elevated heart rate returns to baseline. Every dizzy spell ends. Your body knows how to regulate itself. You just have to let it.

I know this sounds simple. Maybe too simple. You might be thinking, *I've tried noticing my sensations before, and it didn't help. If anything, it made me more anxious.*

And yes, there's a difference between the hypervigilant body-scanning you've probably been doing—that constant checking, that anxious monitoring—and the kind of observation I'm talking about here. Hypervigilance is looking for danger. It's scanning for signs that something's wrong. It's bracing against the next attack.

Interoceptive exposure is different. It's curiosity instead of fear. It's saying, *Huh, my heart is beating fast. I wonder what that feels like.* Instead of, *Oh god, my heart is beating fast. This is bad. I need to make it stop.*

It's a subtle shift, but it matters. One reinforces the threat. The other diffuses it.

Will it be uncomfortable? Absolutely. Will it feel scary at first? Probably. Will you want to quit? Almost certainly.

But here's what I can tell you from working with hundreds of people through this process: it works. Not perfectly. Not permanently. But it works well enough that you can start reclaiming the parts of your life you've been holding back from.

Rachel eats solid food now. She still gets anxious sometimes when she swallows. But she doesn't let that stop her from going to restaurants, from traveling, from living her life. I still notice my heart rate sometimes. I still have moments of anxiety. But I don't organize my entire existence around avoiding those moments anymore. I don't check my pulse fifty times a day. I don't wear the fitness tracker. I go for runs because I want to, not because I'm testing myself.

Your body isn't the enemy. It's not broken. It's not malfunctioning. It's doing exactly what it's supposed to do—trying to keep you safe. The problem is that its threat-detection system has become overly sensitive, and the way to recalibrate it isn't through avoidance or control. It's through gentle, repeated exposure to the very sensations you've been running from.

You don't need to fight your body. You just need to stop treating it like a bomb that might go off at any second.

One last thing. When you start doing this work, you might notice the sensations you were so afraid of might actually intensify at first. This isn't a sign that you're doing it wrong. It's a sign that you're finally paying attention to things you've been avoiding. It's like turning on a light in a dark room—suddenly you can see all the dust and clutter you couldn't see before. That doesn't mean there's more dust. It just means you're finally looking.

So start small. Pick one exercise. Do it once today. Then again tomorrow. Build slowly. Be patient with yourself. Remember that your nervous system didn't learn this pattern overnight, and it won't unlearn it overnight either.

But it *will* learn. Because that's what nervous systems do. They adapt. They recalibrate. They learn new patterns.

Right now, your pattern is: sensation equals danger. With practice, your pattern can become: sensation equals information. Just data. Just your body doing its thing.

And once you can sit with these sensations—once you can feel your heart race without immediately catastrophizing, once you can feel dizzy without assuming you're about to pass out—you'll have something even more powerful than calm.

You'll have resilience.

You'll have proof that you can handle discomfort. That you can be afraid and still be okay.

Let me tell you about one more person, because I think this illustrates something important about how this process actually unfolds in real life—not in a clean, linear way, but messily, with setbacks and breakthroughs all tangled up together.

A client I'll call David came to me after developing a fear of his own heartbeat. Not just a fast heartbeat—any awareness of his heartbeat at all. He'd be lying in bed at night, trying to fall asleep, and he'd become aware of his heart beating in his chest. Just the normal, steady thump of a healthy heart doing its job. And that awareness would trigger immediate panic.

He started sleeping sitting up in a recliner because lying flat made his heartbeat more noticeable. He stopped exercising entirely. He avoided quiet rooms. He kept the TV on constantly for distraction. His entire life became organized around not noticing his own pulse.

When I first suggested interoceptive exposure—having him deliberately focus on his heartbeat—he looked at me with genuine horror. "That's the thing I'm most afraid of. Why would I do that on purpose?"

And that's the paradox at the heart of this work. The thing you're most afraid of is exactly what you need to approach. Not because facing your fears is noble or character-building, but because avoidance is what keeps the fear alive.

We started so small it felt almost silly. I had him place his hand over his heart for five seconds. Just rest it there. Feel the beat. Then take his hand away.

Five seconds. That's all he could tolerate at first.

But we built from there. Five seconds became ten became thirty. Eventually, he could sit for several minutes with his hand over his heart, feeling each beat, without panicking. And as his tolerance grew, something else happened: the sensation became ordinary again. Not pleasant, necessarily, but not threatening. Just information. Just his body, doing what bodies do.

The breakthrough came about two months in. He was lying in bed one night, and he became aware of his heartbeat. The old panic started to rise—but then, instead of immediately reaching for his phone or turning on the TV or getting up to pace around, he just... let it be there. He felt his heart beating. He noticed the panic rising. And he stayed with both sensations, curious about what would happen next.

And what happened was: nothing. The panic peaked, hovered there for maybe thirty seconds, then started to fade. His heartbeat continued, steady and calm, the whole time. By the time he actually fell asleep—lying flat, for the first time in months—he'd spent maybe five minutes just listening to his own pulse. Not fighting it. Not fearing it. Just listening.

He sent me a text the next morning: "I fell asleep listening to my heart. It was weird. But also kind of... peaceful?"

That's the shift I'm talking about. Not from fear to calm, necessarily, but from fear to curiosity. From threat to neutrality. From *this sensation means I'm dying* to *this sensation means I'm alive.*

Now, I want to be clear about something. This work isn't always this neat. There will be days when you do the exercise and it feels manageable, and days when you do the exact same exercise and it feels overwhelming. There will be times when you think you've made progress, and then you have a setback that makes you feel like you're back at square one.

That's normal. That's part of the process. Progress in recovery from panic isn't linear. It's more like a spiral—you come back around to the same challenges, but each time from a slightly different angle, with slightly more capacity.

What I'm asking you to do here is hard. I know that. I'm asking you to deliberately evoke the very sensations that terrify you. I'm asking you to sit with discomfort instead of running from it. I'm asking you to trust a process that feels, at first, completely counterintuitive.

But here's what I'm not asking you to do: I'm not asking you to be brave. I'm not asking you to push through fear. I'm not asking you to white-knuckle your way through exercises that feel unbearable.

I'm asking you to be curious. To approach these sensations with the same kind of neutral observation you might bring to watching clouds move across the sky. Not good, not bad, just there. Changing. Temporary.

And I'm asking you to start small enough that it feels doable. If holding your breath for ten seconds feels like too much, hold it for three. If spinning in a chair feels terrifying, just turn your head side to side and notice the mild dizziness that creates. If running in place to elevate your heart rate feels impossible, just stand up and sit down a few times and notice what that does to your pulse.

The exercises themselves aren't magic. The magic—if we can call it that—is in what happens to your nervous system when you prove to it, over and over, that these sensations aren't dangerous. That you can feel them and survive. That they peak and pass on their own, without you having to do anything to make them go away.

Your nervous system is incredibly adaptable. Right now, it's adapted to treat normal bodily sensations as threats. But it can adapt in the other direction too. It can learn that a racing heart is just a racing heart. That breathlessness is just breathlessness. That dizziness is just dizziness.

None of these sensations are comfortable. But comfortable and safe aren't the same thing. You can be uncomfortable and still be safe. You can be anxious and still be safe. You can feel all the physical symptoms of panic and still be safe.

That's what interoceptive exposure teaches. Not through reassurance, not through logic, but through direct, repeated experience.

And once your body knows—really knows, at a nervous-system level—that these sensations aren't dangerous, everything else gets easier. Not because the sensations disappear, but because they stop controlling your life.

You start making decisions based on what you want to do, not on what you're afraid might trigger a panic attack. You stop checking and monitoring and bracing. You stop living in that constant state of vigilance. You get to just... be in your body again, without treating every flutter and twinge like a five-alarm fire.

So here's what I want you to do. Not tomorrow, not next week, but today. Right now, if you can.

Pick one sensation. Just one. The one that scares you most, or the one that seems most manageable—whichever feels right to you. Then find a simple, safe way to evoke that sensation for a very short period of time.

Maybe it's holding your breath for five seconds. Maybe it's standing up quickly and noticing the brief rush of lightheadedness. Maybe it's doing ten jumping jacks and feeling your heart rate pick up.

Do the exercise. Notice what you feel. Then—and this is the part that matters—don't immediately try to make the sensation go away. Just sit with it for ten seconds. Count them if you need to. One, two, three... all the way to ten. Let the sensation be there. Let yourself notice it without trying to fix it.

Then, if you need to, use whatever coping strategies help you feel safe. Take some deep breaths. Distract yourself. Do whatever you need to do.

But give yourself those ten seconds first. Ten seconds of just noticing, without intervening.

That's where this starts. Not with hours of exposure. Not with pushing yourself to the edge of your tolerance. Just ten seconds of curiosity instead of fear.

Ten seconds of treating the sensation as information instead of threat.

Ten seconds of proving to your nervous system that you can feel uncomfortable and still be okay.

Because here's what you're going to discover, if you keep at this: those ten seconds get easier. And then you can stretch them to twenty. Then thirty. Then a minute. Then several minutes. And somewhere in that process, the sensation that once felt like the most dangerous thing in the world starts to feel like just another bodily experience. Unpleasant, maybe. Unwelcome, sure. But not dangerous. Not worth organizing your entire life around avoiding.

That's the shift. That's what we're working toward.

But noticing the sensations and sitting with them is only half the picture. Because what you do with your breath while all this is happening—whether you're gasping, holding, forcing it, or finding some kind of rhythm that actually helps instead of just masking what's underneath—that's where the real work gets interesting. You can teach your body that a racing heart doesn't mean danger. But that lesson won't hold unless you also know what your breath is doing when your heart isn't racing. When nothing is wrong. When you're just sitting in a quiet room, noticing what calm actually feels like in your chest, underneath all the monitoring and checking and fear.

So let's talk about baseline. Because most people who've lived with panic or health anxiety for any length of time genuinely do not know what their body feels like when it's calm. They know what it feels like when it's ramping up. They know the early warning signs, the subtle shifts that mean something bad might be coming. They've cataloged those in extraordinary detail. But calm? Actual, ordinary, nothing-happening calm? That's foreign territory.

You might think you know. You might say, "Sure, when I'm relaxed, my body feels fine." But if I asked you to describe what "fine" actually feels like—the specific sensations in your chest, the quality of your breathing, the weight of your arms, the temperature of your hands—you'd probably struggle. Because you've spent so long scanning for what's wrong that you've never really mapped what's right.

And that's a problem. Because interoceptive exposure isn't just about facing feared sensations. It's about learning to recognize the difference between a sensation that signals threat and a sensation that's just… a sensation. And you can't do that if you don't have a reference point. If every twinge, every flutter, every shift in rhythm gets filtered through the same threat-detection system, then everything feels dangerous. There's no contrast. No way to tell whether what you're feeling right now is actually different from what you felt ten minutes ago when nothing was wrong.

So part of this work is building that reference point. Sitting down when you're not in crisis—when your heart isn't pounding, when your chest isn't tight, when you're not convinced something terrible is about to happen—and just noticing. What does your breath feel like right now? Not how fast it is, not whether it's "good enough," but what it actually feels like. Is it shallow? Deep? Smooth? A little ragged? Where do you feel it most—your chest, your belly, your throat? And what about your heartbeat? Can you feel it without pressing your fingers to your wrist or your neck? Is it steady? Does it seem loud, or is it just there in the background?

This isn't meditation in the sense of trying to achieve some blissed-out state. It's data collection. You're learning what normal feels like in your body, so that when something shifts, you have a baseline to compare it to. And more importantly, so that when you deliberately trigger a sensation during exposure—when you spin in a chair or breathe fast or tense your muscles—you can recognize when it starts to settle back down. You can notice, "Oh, that's what my breath does when it's calming. That's what my heart sounds like when it's not in overdrive anymore." Without that baseline, recovery feels invisible. You might be coming down from activation, but if you don't know what "down" feels like, you'll keep scanning, keep waiting for proof that you're safe, and miss the fact that your body is already giving it to you.

And here's the uncomfortable part: building that baseline requires you to stop doing all the things you normally do to feel safe. The checking. The reassurance-seeking. The mental calculations about whether this sensation is normal or whether you need to do something about it. Because all of that—no matter how automatic it's become—pulls you out of the actual experience of your body and into your head, where you're analyzing and comparing and trying to determine if you're okay. And as long as you're doing that, you're not really feeling anything. You're just monitoring.

There's a difference. Monitoring is when you're scanning for danger. Feeling is when you're noticing what's actually there. Monitoring has an agenda: to confirm that you're safe or to catch a threat before it becomes unmanageable. Feeling doesn't have an agenda. It's just observation. And it turns out that most of the sensations people with health anxiety are terrified of aren't actually that intense when you're just feeling them. They're only unbearable when you're also layering on the fear, the interpretation, the story about what it means.

So when you sit with your breath, when you notice your heartbeat, when you pay attention to the physical sensations in your body without immediately jumping to conclusions about them—you're practicing that shift. From monitoring to feeling. From threat detection to simple awareness. And that shift is what makes interoceptive exposure possible. Because you can't habituate to a sensation you're not actually experiencing. If you're too busy analyzing it, catastrophizing about it, trying to make it go away—you're not in contact with it. You're in contact with your fear of it. And fear doesn't habituate to fear. It just spirals.

But when you can sit with the sensation itself—the actual tightness in your chest, the actual flutter in your stomach, the actual shakiness in your hands—without the story, without the panic, without the need to make it stop right now—that's when something starts to shift. Not because the sensation goes away, but because you start to realize it doesn't have to. It can be there, uncomfortable and unwanted, and you can be okay. Not happy about it. Not pretending it doesn't bother you. Just… okay. Still breathing. Still here. Still safe, even though it doesn't feel like it.

And once that happens—once you've had even one experience of sitting with a feared sensation and coming out the other side without collapsing, without ending up in the emergency room, without your worst fear coming true—you've cracked the door open. Because now you know it's possible. It's not theoretical anymore. It's not something your therapist told you or something you read in a book. It's something you lived through. And that changes everything.

That fleeting moment between startle and rationalization is precisely what interoceptive exposure aims to recapture—a space where sensation isn't immediately labeled as threatening.

Chapter 5: Breathing as a Tool, Not a Cure

I was watching David try to describe his first panic attack, but what held my attention wasn't the story itself—the usual catalogue of racing heart, tunnel vision, the certainty he was dying—it was his hands. White knuckles around a chipped ceramic mug that had gone cold twenty minutes ago. And his chest: this careful, deliberate rise and fall.

He was trying to control his breathing before the panic even arrived. Preemptive damage control.

I'd seen this hundreds of times across fifteen years of practice. Client sits down, tells me about the tightness in their chest, the dizzy spells, the hyperventilation—and while they're talking, they're already doing it. Deep, intentional inhales. Slow, measured exhales. An internal thermostat permanently set to "appear calm." Most people didn't even realize they were doing it. They just assumed that anxiety meant broken breathing. That every shift in respiratory rhythm needed immediate correction.

And look—breathwork has a place. We'll get there. But this reflexive attempt to manually regulate every fluctuation in your breath? It doesn't calm your nervous system. It teaches your nervous system that ordinary sensations are dangerous. That your body can't be trusted. That you need constant surveillance just to stay alive.

Here's the thing your body is actually doing when panic hits. You perceive a threat—real, imagined, doesn't matter—and your sympathetic nervous system activates. Adrenaline floods your bloodstream. Your breathing accelerates and gets shallow, pulling oxygen to your limbs instead of your digestive system because digestion is spectacularly unimportant when you're about to get eaten by a tiger.

This isn't a glitch. It's evolution.

That breathless feeling everyone hates? It's blood being diverted from leisurely activities like processing lunch and sent to muscles primed for action. Your body is doing exactly what it's supposed to do. Trying to override this deeply embedded survival response in real-time isn't just ineffective—it's like fighting yourself. Which only amplifies the sense of threat.

Think about holding a beach ball underwater. You push down. It fights back. You push harder. It fights harder. You're burning through oxygen, your muscles are screaming, and eventually your body demands air and the ball rockets to the surface anyway.

You can't win.

Trying to force "perfect" breathing during panic works the same way. All you're doing is intensifying your focus on breath itself—turning it into the enemy when it's actually just one neutral signal among thousands your body is sending every moment.

Let me tell you what that constant vigilance actually costs. Not in some abstract intellectual sense, but in real, daily wreckage.

You wake up already scanning. Before your feet touch the floor, before you're even fully conscious, you're running diagnostics: Is my breathing normal? Does my chest feel tight? Is my heart racing?

You get to work. Someone asks you a question and you realize you didn't hear a single word because you were monitoring whether your breathing looked normal, whether anyone could tell you were focusing on it.

You're in a meeting and your mind isn't on the presentation—it's on whether your breath is too fast, too shallow, too loud. You start tracking the rhythm of your inhales against the rhythm of whoever's speaking. You wonder if the person next to you can hear you breathing. You try to make it quieter. Which, of course, makes you more breathless. Which makes you panic more.

You start avoiding. No running to catch the train because that'll spike your heart rate. No laughing too hard at lunch because that might trigger breathlessness. No dancing, no sex that gets your heart pumping, because if your breathing speeds up you'll have to control it, manage it, fix it.

You're working two full-time jobs now. Your actual job, and Chief Respiratory Officer of your own body.

And you're exhausted.

Not just physically tired, though that too. You're exhausted from the vigilance. From the constant inner monologue: *Am I breathing right? Is this normal? Should I be worried about this? Was that breath too shallow?*

Underneath all of it—and this is the part nobody wants to say out loud—there's this creeping sense of failure. Because no matter how hard you try, you can't seem to get it *right*. Your breath won't stay perfectly controlled. Your body keeps doing what bodies do, which is respond to stress and effort and emotion, and every time it does you feel like you're losing.

That's what I saw in David's white knuckles that day. Not just anxiety. Exhaustion. The bone-deep weariness of someone who'd been trying to manually override his own nervous system for six months straight.

Panic happens when your body misinterprets neutral stimuli as threats. Your amygdala, the brain's alarm center, fires. That triggers a cascade of responses designed to keep you alive: rapid breathing, racing heart, tunnel vision. In the moment it feels catastrophic.

But it's not.

It's your overprotective security system doing exactly what it was designed to do, just at the wrong time. The smoke detector going off because you burned toast, not because the house is on fire.

What that meant for me, early in my clinical practice, was this: I taught clients to "control" their breathing during panic. Four counts in, hold for two, six counts out. It felt evidence-based. Scientific. Longer exhales activate the parasympathetic nervous system, the "rest and digest" response. I'd walk people through the technique, watch them practice it in session, send them home with instructions.

I thought I was helping people manage their symptoms.

I thought that *was* the work.

Then I met Sarah. Graphic designer, thirty-four, social anxiety that had cost her three promotions because she couldn't present to clients without her hands shaking so badly she'd spill her coffee. We were in my office, third session, and she'd just finished describing another failed presentation. She'd used the breathing technique. Multiple times. It hadn't helped.

And she looked at me with this expression I still remember—not angry, not even particularly frustrated, just… defeated—and she said: "If I need to control my breath for the rest of my life to feel safe, have I really recovered?"

I sat there.

I didn't have an answer.

Because she was right. I'd been teaching management, not recovery. I'd been handing people tools to fight their own bodies, then calling it treatment. Every time I taught that four-count breath, I was reinforcing the idea that their natural physiological response was the enemy. That they couldn't be trusted. That safety required constant intervention.

Sarah's question dismantled five years of my training in about eight seconds.

What I was offering wasn't freedom. It was just a more sophisticated version of the same underlying fear: that their bodies were broken and needed fixing. I was giving them a lifetime subscription to vigilance.

That conversation changed how I practice.

Because here's what I understand now: recovery doesn't mean eliminating panic symptoms. It means changing your relationship to those sensations. Not making them disappear—learning to stop treating a racing heart like an emergency when it's really just your security system misfiring.

So what's the alternative to constant control?

It's not about achieving some idealized state of perfect, calm respiration. It's about finding your baseline rhythm. Your natural breathing pattern when you're genuinely at rest—not performing rest, not trying to look calm, but actually just… existing. Not a "good" breath or a "correct" one. Just *your* breath, as it is, right now.

And acknowledging that fluctuations are normal. Inevitable. Not dangerous.

One way to access this—and notice I'm saying "access," not "achieve," because it's already there, you're just learning to recognize it—is through breath awareness. Which is different from breath control. The difference matters more than almost anything else I'm going to tell you in this chapter.

Find a comfortable position. Sitting works. Lying down works. Standing, if that's what you've got. Close your eyes if that feels safe, or just soften your gaze toward the floor. And then notice your breath.

Don't change it. Don't judge it. Don't fix it.

Just feel the air entering your nostrils, filling your lungs, leaving your body. Notice the rise and fall of your chest or abdomen. The temperature of the air coming in versus going out. The tiny pause between inhale and exhale.

Your mind will wander. Guaranteed. That's not failure—that's what minds do. When you notice it wandering, just redirect your attention back to the sensation of breathing. Not with frustration. Not with self-criticism. Just: back.

Like you're gently picking up a puppy that wandered off and placing it back on the rug. No drama. Just redirection.

This isn't a quick fix. It's not supposed to instantly calm you down or stop panic attacks. That's the whole point—it's not a tool you're wielding *against* your anxiety. It's a practice of getting familiar with your body's baseline so that when things shift, you recognize the shift for what it is: information, not catastrophe.

Over time—weeks, not days—breath awareness helps you desensitize to the physical sensations of anxiety. You start recognizing that even rapid or shallow breaths aren't inherently dangerous. They're just signals. Your body communicating about its state. And because you've practiced observing them without immediately trying to fix them, they lose some of their power to trigger cascading panic.

I worked with a nurse named Amelia. Forty-two, ICU, worked through the worst of the pandemic. She'd been the calm one, the steady hand, the person other nurses looked to when a patient was crashing. Then she had a shift where she lost three patients in one night—not through any error on her part, just the brutal math of a virus that didn't care how good you were—and something broke.

She started experiencing panic attacks. Not at work, interestingly. At home. In the shower, in her car, lying in bed at night.

The intrusive thoughts were the worst part, she said. Physical sensations that mirrored what she'd witnessed in dying patients: the gasping, the chest tightness, the sense of suffocation.

When I first met her, she described being "constantly on high alert." Bracing for the next wave.

"I'm trying to breathe through it," she said, and the frustration in her voice was thick enough to cut. "But it's exhausting. Like I'm working a second job just keeping my own body in check."

She was spending hours each day monitoring her breathing. Forcing slow, deep breaths whenever she felt the slightest hint of discomfort. Even when she wasn't anxious, she was breathing *carefully*. Like her lungs were made of glass and one wrong move would shatter them.

We started with breath awareness. Not to stop the anxiety—to create space around it.

I asked her to simply observe her breathing without trying to change anything. Just notice it. Track it like a scientist, not a judge.

At first she hated it. She kept wanting to "fix" things. But slowly—over weeks of practice—she began noticing that her breath wasn't always erratic. Sometimes it was calm and steady. Other times it was fast and uneven.

Both were okay. Neither required intervention.

She started practicing during small moments throughout her day. While washing dishes. Waiting in line at the grocery store. During her commute. Not trying to achieve calm—just noticing what was there. Building her capacity for self-observation without self-criticism.

The physical sensations didn't disappear. Her heart still raced sometimes. Her breath still quickened. But they stopped feeling like threats. They were signals from her nervous system, information about her state, not evidence that something was fundamentally wrong with her.

The breathlessness wasn't the problem. Her relationship to it was.

This shift—from fearing the sensations to observing them—is where real change starts. But observation alone isn't enough for most people. You also need tools. Specific practices you can turn to when that faster rhythm kicks in, when you feel tension building and you want to do *something* but you know the old pattern of forcing calm doesn't work.

This is where breathwork gets complicated.

Because the way it's usually presented—usually sold, honestly—sets people up for frustration. Breathing techniques aren't magic bullets. They won't instantly eliminate panic. They're not going to make anxiety disappear like some kind of nervous system reset button.

What they can do is help you find your baseline. A comfortable rhythm to return to when things speed up. Not a cure. A tool.

Your nervous system isn't broken. It's responding predictably to perceived threat. Breathing exercises don't override that response—they influence it. Gently. They nudge you back toward your baseline.

Think adjusting the volume on a radio, not yanking out the power cord.

We talk about "calming" the breath, but sometimes that's not what's needed. Sometimes, after a panic attack—or even during the early stages of rising anxiety—your breathing is already too restricted, too shallow. You've been trying so hard to control it that you've strangled it. And trying to force it even slower can feel suffocating.

The goal isn't necessarily slow breathing. It's *balanced* breathing. A rhythm that feels sustainable for you, in this particular moment, given what your body is actually doing right now.

You've probably heard of 4-7-8 breathing. Inhale for four counts, hold for seven, exhale for eight. It can work—the extended exhale does activate your parasympathetic nervous system. But it doesn't work for everyone. Some people find that holding their breath for seven counts increases their sense of panic. Makes them feel trapped.

The key is experimentation. Not adherence to someone else's perfect formula.

Box breathing is another popular one: inhale for four, hold for four, exhale for four, hold for four. The appeal is the symmetry, the equal weight given to each phase. It can create a sense of stability, of groundedness.

But again—it's not universal. What if four counts feels too fast for you? Or too slow? The "box" isn't a fixed container. You can adjust it. Maybe 3-4-5-4 feels better for your nervous system. Maybe 6-6-6-6. Maybe you don't hold at all between breaths because the holding actually creates more tension.

I remember one client, Mark—a high school history teacher with a tendency to catastrophize—tried everything. Four-seven-eight, box breathing, diaphragmatic breathing, alternate nostril breathing. Nothing stuck. He'd get halfway through and his mind would start racing: *Am I doing this right? Is my diaphragm actually moving? What if I hyperventilate?*

Then he stumbled upon a technique almost by accident. While gardening—he took it up as a way to de-stress, ironically—he started paying attention to the natural rhythm of his breath while weeding. Not trying to change it. Just noticing how it rose and fell in sync with the physical exertion.

He realized that when he was focused on the task at hand—pulling weeds, feeling the dirt between his fingers—his breathing naturally slowed down and deepened. It wasn't about forcing anything. It was about finding an activity that engaged his body and mind enough to allow his breath to regulate itself.

He started incorporating little bursts of physical activity into his day: a brisk walk during lunch break, doing jumping jacks between classes, even just stretching at his desk. And he found that those movements, combined with mindful awareness, were far more effective than any prescribed breathing technique.

His baseline wasn't four-seven-eight. It was weeding. It was walking. It was *moving.*

And that's the lesson here: your baseline isn't a number. It's not a ratio of inhale to exhale. It's the state of relaxed alertness you experience when you're fully engaged in life, when your nervous system feels safe and supported.

It's remembering what it felt like before you started scanning for threats. Before you started bracing for panic. Before you turned your breath into an enemy.

Finding that baseline requires curiosity. Experimentation. And a willingness to ditch the idea of "perfect" breathing altogether.

Start small. Spend five minutes each day simply observing your breath. No judgment, no fixing, just noticing. Pay attention to how it changes throughout the day—how it shifts with different activities, emotions, and levels of stress.

Then start experimenting with gentle movements that feel good in your body. Walking, stretching, yoga, dancing, gardening. Anything that gets you out of your head and into your physical sensations.

Notice how those movements affect your breath. Do they help it slow down? Deepen? Become more balanced?

Over time—and this takes consistent practice—you'll begin to develop a deeper awareness of your body's natural rhythms. You'll learn to recognize when your breathing is becoming dysregulated and you'll have a toolbox of techniques to gently guide it back toward balance.

You won't eliminate anxiety. That's not the goal, and frankly, it's not realistic. Life *is* stressful. Things will happen that trigger your nervous system. The key isn't to avoid those triggers—it's to learn how to respond to them with more flexibility and resilience.

And maybe, just maybe, you'll start realizing something truly profound: that your body isn't the enemy. It's a remarkably intelligent system, constantly adapting to its environment, doing everything it can to keep you safe.

It deserves your curiosity, not your control. Your compassion, not your judgment. And a deep, unwavering trust in its inherent ability to heal and regulate itself.

David's rigid control over his breathing reveals the paradox of trying to *force* calm, suggesting a need for a more nuanced approach that honors the body's natural rhythms.

Chapter 6: Grounding Techniques

Five smooth stones in a velvet pouch. A piece of peppermint gum. A credit card-sized laminated list with eight words on it.

These are the objects people have shown me when I asked what they carry for panic—their lifelines, their anchors, their ways back to solid ground when everything else feels like it's dissolving.

These are the objects people have shown me when I asked what they carry for panic—their lifelines, their anchors, their ways back to solid ground when everything else feels like it's dissolving. I've seen stranger things. A woman once showed me a tiny snow globe, the kind you'd find in a gas station gift shop, with a plastic palm tree inside. A man carried a guitar pick even though he'd never played guitar in his life. He just liked the way it felt between his thumb and forefinger, the slight flex when he pressed down, the beveled edge catching under his nail.

I don't think any of them expected these objects to *cure* anything. But they needed something to grab onto. Something real. Something that existed outside the closed loop of their own spiraling thoughts.

I get that. Because I spent forty-five minutes in a CVS parking lot once, gripping my steering wheel like it was the only solid thing left in the universe, with absolutely nothing to hold onto except my own terror.

The attack itself had passed—the crushing chest pressure, the tunnel vision, the absolute certainty I was dying. What hadn't passed was the aftermath.

I'd started cataloging every sensation. A flutter in my chest while reaching for cereal became a medical emergency. A moment of dizziness standing up too quickly turned into thirty minutes of frantic Googling. I was living inside my body like it was a house I no longer trusted, checking every creak and groan for signs of structural collapse.

That Tuesday, I was sitting in my car after picking up a prescription—nothing serious, just allergy medication—when I felt my heart skip.

Just once.

A tiny blip most people wouldn't notice.

But I noticed. And the moment I noticed, my attention locked onto it like a heat-seeking missile. *Is it doing it again? Yes—there. Another skip. Oh god, this is it. This is the big one.*

Within thirty seconds I was in free fall. Heart rate climbing. Breath shallow and fast. Vision narrowing. The entire world reduced to the question: *Am I dying right now?*

Here's what nobody tells you about that state—when you're that deep inside your own physiological alarm system, there's nowhere to grab hold. It's like trying to stop a fall when there's nothing around you but air. You're untethered, spinning, and every attempt to regain control just sends you deeper into the spiral because *trying to control it* is itself a form of panic.

I didn't have a second panic attack that day. But I sat in that parking lot for forty-five minutes, unable to move. Not because I was physically incapable—my body was fine, just activated and buzzing—but because I had no anchor. Nothing to tie me back to the present moment, to the fact that I was safe, that this would pass, that my racing heart was just my nervous system being overzealous, not a cardiac event.

What I needed, and didn't have, was a way to interrupt the inward spiral.

Not to stop the sensations—you can't just turn off an activated nervous system like flipping a light switch—but to shift my attention *alongside* them instead of being consumed by them. To create some breathing room between the panic and my awareness of it.

That's what grounding does. And before we get into the how, I need you to understand the cost of not having it. Because that cost is what you're living with right now, whether you've named it or not.

Here's what happens when you don't know how to ground yourself: you become a hostage to your own nervous system.

Every sensation gets interrogated. Is this normal? Is this dangerous? Should I call someone? The vigilance is exhausting, but you can't stop because stopping feels like letting your guard down, and letting your guard down feels like inviting disaster. So you start avoiding situations that might trigger symptoms. Crowded places. Exercise. Caffeine. Long drives. Anything that might make your heart beat faster or your breath quicken.

Your world gets smaller and smaller, but you tell yourself it's worth it because at least you're safe.

Except you're not safer.

You're just more afraid.

The physiological reality is this: hypervigilance keeps your nervous system in a low-grade state of activation. You're never fully relaxed because you're always scanning for threat. And a nervous system that's chronically activated is *more* likely to tip into panic, not less. It's like keeping your car engine revving constantly—eventually something's going to overheat.

But the psychological cost is worse.

When you can't anchor yourself in the present moment, you lose access to your own life. You're physically *in* the coffee shop with your friend, but mentally you're three steps ahead, catastrophizing about whether the tightness in your chest means something terrible. You're at your kid's soccer game but you're not watching them play—you're monitoring your heartbeat. You're in bed next to your partner but you're Googling symptoms on your phone instead of sleeping.

I did this for months. Sat through dinners I couldn't taste. Drove routes I couldn't remember afterward because I'd spent the entire drive checking whether my breathing felt wrong. Had conversations where I nodded at the right moments but couldn't tell you a single thing the other person said because I was too busy taking my own pulse.

That's not living. That's just being alive while panic runs the show.

And here's the thing that made it worse: I *knew* I was doing it. I could see myself disappearing into this hypervigilant fog, could watch my own life shrinking, and I still couldn't stop. Because I didn't have a tool. I had willpower, which is useless against an activated nervous system. I had rational thoughts, which panic doesn't care about. I had good intentions, which might as well have been prayers for all the good they did.

What I didn't have was a concrete, repeatable way to pull my attention out of the tailspin and put it somewhere else.

Recovery isn't about eliminating panic symptoms. It's about learning to stay *present* with them, to acknowledge them without letting them hijack your entire experience. And that requires a skill most of us don't naturally have: the ability to deliberately shift our focus from the internal storm to the external world.

Which sounds simple. And in some ways, it is.

But simple and easy are not the same thing.

Physiologically speaking, what's happening during that inward spiral is a narrowing of attention.

Your pupils dilate. Your peripheral vision constricts. Blood flow redirects away from non-essential functions—digestion, creative thinking, broad awareness—and toward the muscles and organs needed for fight or flight. This is an evolutionary feature, not a bug. When our ancestors faced actual predators, tunnel vision helped them focus on the immediate threat. Noticing the beautiful sunset or the texture of tree bark would have gotten them killed.

But here's the problem: that same mechanism activates when the "threat" is just your own racing heart or a wave of dizziness.

Your attention narrows to the sensation itself, which amplifies it, which narrows your attention further. Feedback loop. The more you focus on your heart rate, the more alarming it becomes. The more alarming it becomes, the more your heart rate increases. Round and round.

What that meant for me—and what it might mean for you—is that breaking the loop requires something almost paradoxical. You have to deliberately *broaden* your focus at the exact moment when your entire system is screaming at you to narrow it. You have to actively look outward when every instinct says look inward.

Grounding techniques work because they hijack your attention in a specific, structured way. They force you to engage with immediate sensory input—things you can see, hear, touch, smell, taste—which activates different neural pathways than the ones firing during panic.

You literally cannot simultaneously catalogue five things you can see in your environment *and* catastrophize about your heart rate. The brain doesn't multitask that way. One process interrupts the other.

It's not magic. It's just neurology. But knowing the mechanism doesn't make it less effective—it just helps you trust it when your anxiety is telling you that nothing will work.

The most well-known grounding technique is the 5-4-3-2-1 method, and if it sounds too simple to work, I understand the skepticism.

I had the same reaction the first time someone suggested it. *You want me to just... notice things? That's supposed to stop a panic attack?*

Not stop. Interrupt.

Here's how it works: you name five things you can see, four things you can touch, three things you can hear, two things you can smell, and one thing you can taste. The structure matters—the descending numbers create a gentle deceleration, a slowing down of frantic energy. And the specificity matters. Not just "a chair," but "a wooden chair with a scuff mark on the left leg." Not "fabric," but "the rough weave of this blanket, slightly pilled near the edge."

The detail is the point.

You're not trying to *think* your way out of panic—that doesn't work. You're redirecting your sensory attention to verifiable, external facts. Things that exist whether you're anxious about them or not.

Let me show you what this looks like in practice, because the first time I watched someone actually use it, I understood why it worked.

Marcus is a software engineer, thirty-four, who had his first panic attack during a code review meeting. Now, even opening his laptop sometimes triggers a wave of anticipatory anxiety—heart racing, breath shallow, vision slightly blurred. He's started dreading work, which terrifies him because he loves his job. Or he did, before his body decided that work equals danger.

One morning he's sitting at his desk, coffee cooling beside him, and he feels it starting.

The familiar tightness in his chest. The thought: *Oh no, not again.* And then the cascade: *What if I can't work anymore? What if this ruins my career? What if—*

He catches himself. We'd talked about this moment—the fork in the road where he could either follow the spiral down or try something different. He closes his eyes briefly, then opens them and starts with the first step.

Five things he can see.

"The blue Post-it note stuck to my monitor. The coffee ring on my desk—brown, uneven. The charging cable, black, coiled. That plant Sarah gave me, the one I keep forgetting to water. The crack in the wall near the window, running diagonal."

He doesn't rush. He really looks. The Post-it isn't just blue—it's that specific sky blue, slightly faded at one corner. The plant isn't just a plant—it's got three leaves, one curling at the tip, soil dry at the surface.

Four things he can touch.

He reaches out.

"The cool ceramic of the coffee mug." He wraps his hands around it, noticing the temperature, the smooth glaze, the slight ridge where the handle attaches. "The wooden desk—smooth here, rough where it's chipped." He runs his finger along the grain. "The fabric of my shirt, soft, worn." He pinches the material between his fingers. "My watch, metal, a little warm from my skin." He rotates his wrist, feeling the weight shift.

Three things he can hear.

This is harder. His heart is loud in his ears. But he listens past it.

"The hum of my computer fan—low, constant. Someone's phone vibrating in the other room—short bursts. Traffic outside, distant, white noise."

Two things he can smell.

"Coffee, obviously. And... something like dust? Or maybe the faint chemical smell of the keyboard cleaner."

One thing he can taste.

He takes a small sip of coffee. "Bitter. A little burnt because I made it too early."

The whole process takes maybe ninety seconds.

And when he finishes, the anxiety hasn't vanished. His heart is still beating faster than normal. There's still tightness in his chest. But something's shifted. The panic isn't *smaller*, exactly—it's just... alongside him now instead of swallowing him whole. He can feel it, acknowledge it, and still be aware of the coffee cup, the desk, the hum of the fan.

He opens his email. Responds to a message. The anxiety fades gradually over the next ten minutes, but not because he fought it. Because he stopped feeding it his complete attention.

That's the mechanism. Attention redirection.

Simple, not easy.

And like any skill, it gets better with practice. Which brings me to something important: don't wait for panic to try it.

(You might be thinking: *But if I practice it when I'm calm, how will I know it works when I'm anxious?* Fair question. Answer: because building the neural pathway when you're calm makes it accessible when you're not. It's muscle memory. You're teaching your brain a route it can follow automatically when conscious decision-making is compromised.)

Try it right now. Wherever you are.

Five things you can see. Don't just list them—really *look*. Notice color, shape, texture, light and shadow. What's in your peripheral vision? What did you not notice until you actively paid attention?

Four things you can touch. Reach out. Feel the difference between smooth and rough, warm and cool, soft and hard. Your body is constantly receiving tactile information—you're just not usually aware of it. This exercise makes it conscious.

Three things you can hear. Close your eyes if it helps. What's the quietest sound in your environment? What's constant? What's intermittent? Can you separate individual sounds from the general background noise?

Two things you can smell. This one often surprises people. We tune out smell quickly—it's called olfactory adaptation. But if you actively sniff, you'll notice things. Coffee, fabric softener, your own skin, the faint mustiness of an old book.

One thing you can taste. Even if you haven't eaten recently, there's usually something—residual toothpaste, the inside of your mouth, a sip of water.

The first time feels mechanical. That's normal. You're learning a new pattern, and new patterns feel artificial before they feel natural.

Stick with it. Do it daily for a week. In the morning while you're drinking coffee. On your commute. Before bed. The more you practice, the more automatic it becomes, and the easier it is to access when your nervous system is in overdrive.

I'll be honest: the first week I practiced this, I felt ridiculous. Sitting in my kitchen naming objects like a kindergartener learning vocabulary. *Spoon. Shiny. Cold.* But I kept doing it because I was desperate enough to try anything, and after about ten days something clicked. I stopped thinking about the technique itself and started just... noticing. The world got sharper. More textured. I'd been so trapped in my own head for so long that I'd forgotten what it felt like to actually *be* in a room instead of just physically occupying it.

Some people prefer a tangible toolkit—a curated collection of objects with distinct sensory qualities.

I'm one of them.

I keep a small zippered pouch in my bag: a smooth river stone, a square of velvet fabric, a tiny vial of peppermint oil, and a guitar pick. (I don't play guitar. I just like the texture—the slight flex when I press my thumbnail against it, the beveled edge.)

The logic is the same as the 5-4-3-2-1 technique—sensory engagement to interrupt spiraling thoughts—but instead of scanning your environment, you're engaging with specific, pre-selected objects. This is useful when your environment isn't particularly grounding. Fluorescent-lit waiting rooms. Crowded subway cars. That CVS parking lot where I spent forty-five minutes stuck in my own head.

Building a grounding kit isn't about accumulating beautiful things. It's about identifying what genuinely captures your sensory attention. Not what *should* work, but what actually *does* work for you.

For tactile grounding, smooth stones are popular because they're cool, weighted, and have texture variations if you pay attention. But maybe you prefer something softer—a scrap of velvet, a worn cotton handkerchief, a small stress ball. Or something with more resistance—a Rubik's cube, a spring, a piece of Velcro you can pull apart and press back together. The point isn't the object itself; it's whether manipulating it pulls you out of your head and into your hands.

Scent is powerful because it bypasses a lot of cognitive processing. It hits the limbic system—the part of your brain involved in emotion and memory—directly. Lavender and chamomile are classic choices, but don't force it if floral scents don't resonate. Peppermint, citrus, cedarwood, even coffee beans—whatever reliably anchors your attention. A tiny vial is enough. You don't need much.

For sound, some people carry small chimes, tuning forks, or have specific playlists on their phones—nature sounds, instrumental music, even recordings of loved ones' voices. The content matters less than the ability to focus on it.

Visual grounding can be as simple as a photograph, a patterned stone, a small kaleidoscope. Something you can look at closely, noticing details you'd miss at a glance.

The whole kit should fit in a small pouch—pocket-sized, portable.

This isn't about creating a cumbersome ritual. It's about having reliable tools accessible before you're completely overwhelmed.

I met Jenna in a support group about eight months after my CVS parking lot incident. She'd had her first panic attack on a plane—turbulence, middle seat, no escape—and now she couldn't travel without intense anticipatory anxiety. She'd started turning down work trips, avoiding family visits, canceling vacations. Her world was shrinking.

We talked about grounding kits. She was skeptical.

"A bag of rocks and some essential oil is supposed to fix this?"

"Not fix. Interrupt," I said.

She built one anyway. Not rocks—she hated the cold, smooth texture. Instead: a small piece of faux fur (tactile), a vial of eucalyptus oil (scent), and a photograph of her dog (visual). Simple. Portable. Hers.

A month later, she took a short flight—just an hour, a trial run.

Sitting in the terminal, waiting to board, she felt the familiar dread building. Heart rate climbing. Breath getting shallow. The voice in her head saying *You can't do this. You're going to lose it up there and everyone will see.*

She didn't fight it. She reached into her bag and pulled out the faux fur. Started stroking it, focusing on the softness, the way it moved under her fingers. Opened the eucalyptus oil and inhaled—sharp, clarifying. Looked at the photo of her dog, noticing details she'd somehow never registered before. (A small patch of white on his left paw. The way one ear folded slightly at the tip.)

The anxiety didn't disappear.

But it stopped escalating.

She boarded the plane. Took her seat. Used the grounding kit twice more during the flight—once during takeoff, once when they hit a patch of turbulence. She didn't enjoy the flight. But she got through it.

That's the bar. Not enjoyment. Not even calm. Just *through*.

She travels regularly now. Still uses the kit sometimes, but less often. The goal was never permanent dependence on a bag of objects. It was building the internal capacity to redirect attention, with external tools as training wheels until the skill became automatic.

You might be wondering: *What if grounding doesn't work? What if I try the 5-4-3-2-1 thing and I'm still panicking?*

First, redefine "work."

If you're expecting grounding to make panic vanish instantly, you're setting yourself up for disappointment. That's not how nervous systems operate. Grounding isn't a magic off-switch. It's a redirection tool.

Success looks like this: *I'm still anxious, but I'm not completely consumed by it. I can feel my heart racing and also notice the texture of this fabric. I'm aware of the panic and also aware that I'm sitting in a safe place.*

That dual awareness—*this* is happening, *and* I'm here—is the goal.

Not elimination. Coexistence.

Second, recognize that some moments require more than one tool. If you try 5-4-3-2-1 and you're still spiraling, add something else. Deep breathing—but not hyperventilation, the kind of slow, deliberate breathing we covered earlier. Movement. A short walk, even just standing up and sitting down. Saying something out loud. ("I'm feeling anxious, and that's okay.") These tools stack. They're not mutually exclusive.

Third, understand that grounding works *better* the more you practice it when you're *not* in crisis.

If the first time you try to anchor yourself in the present moment is during a full-blown panic attack, it's like trying to learn to swim while drowning. Possible, but not ideal. Practice when you're calm. Build the pathway. Then when you need it, the route is already there.

I can't count how many times I've done the 5-4-3-2-1 exercise in perfectly safe, calm moments. Sitting on my couch. Eating breakfast. Waiting for my computer to boot up. It felt pointless at the time—*Why am I doing this when I'm not even anxious?*—but those repetitions mattered. They built the neural pathway. So when I *was* anxious, when my prefrontal cortex went offline and rational thought became inaccessible, the grounding sequence was still there. Automatic. Reflexive.

The neuroscience here is worth understanding, even briefly, because it explains why grounding works when so many other interventions don't.

When you're in a state of panic, your prefrontal cortex—the part of your brain responsible for rational thought, planning, decision-making—goes partially offline. Blood flow redirects to the amygdala and other structures involved in the fear response. This is why you can *know* intellectually that you're not in danger and still *feel* like you're dying. The part of your brain that holds rational knowledge isn't running the show.

Grounding works because it doesn't rely on the prefrontal cortex.

It engages sensory processing—sight, sound, touch, smell, taste—which routes through different neural pathways. You're essentially sneaking past the fear response by activating parts of the brain that panic hasn't shut down.

And here's the part that matters for long-term recovery: the more you practice grounding, the more you're teaching your nervous system that panic, while uncomfortable, isn't dangerous. You're building evidence. *I felt anxious, I used grounding, I got through it. The panic peaked and then it passed.*

Over time, that evidence accumulates.

Your nervous system starts to learn that the sensations of panic—racing heart, shallow breath, dizziness—are just sensations. Not threats. Not emergencies. Just your body's overprotective alarm system doing its thing.

This is the shift that matters. Not eliminating panic. Not even reducing its frequency, though that often happens as a side effect. But fundamentally changing your *relationship* to it. Moving from "Oh god, I'm panicking, this is a catastrophe" to "I'm having panic sensations, this is uncomfortable, I know what to do."

There's a moment, early in recovery, when you realize you've been treating your own body like an enemy.

Every flutter, every skip, every moment of dizziness gets interpreted as betrayal. *Why is my body doing this to me?* As if your heart is staging a coup. As if your nervous system is conspiring against you.

But your body isn't trying to hurt you. It's trying to protect you. It's just... overprotective. Overzealous. Like a smoke detector that goes off when you burn toast—annoying, disruptive, but ultimately coming from a place of trying to keep you safe.

Grounding is the first step toward changing that relationship. Not by suppressing the alarm system, but by acknowledging it and then choosing where to put your attention. *Yes, I hear you. Yes, I feel the panic. And also, I'm going to notice these five things I can see.*

It's a different kind of control than the one most of us are reaching for. We want to control *whether* we feel anxious. Grounding teaches us to control *where we focus* while we feel anxious.

That distinction sounds small.

It's not.

Because once you realize you can feel panic *and* stay anchored to the present moment, you stop being afraid of the panic itself. You stop avoiding situations that might trigger it. You stop shrinking your life. You stop checking out of your own experiences because you're too busy monitoring your heartbeat.

You start living again.

Not fearlessly—recovery doesn't mean you'll never feel anxious. But you'll feel anxious *and* keep going. Anxious *and* present. Anxious *and* engaged with your actual life instead of the catastrophic story your mind is spinning.

And that changes everything.

So here's what I want you to do, starting today.

Build your grounding practice now, before you need it. Pick one technique—the 5-4-3-2-1 method, a grounding kit, whatever resonates—and practice it daily for two weeks. Not when you're panicking. When you're calm. When it feels pointless. When you're tempted to skip it because "I'm fine right now."

Do it anyway.

Build the pathway. Teach your nervous system the route. Give yourself a tool that doesn't rely on willpower or rational thought or good intentions.

Because the next time panic shows up—and it will, that's just how recovery works—you'll have something to reach for. Something concrete. Something that works not because it's magical, but because you practiced it enough that it became automatic.

You'll have a way back to solid ground.

And once you know you can find your way back, the panic itself becomes less terrifying. It's still uncomfortable. Still disruptive. But it's no longer the five-alarm fire it used to be. It's just a smoke detector going off because you burned the toast.

Annoying, sure.

But not the end of the world.

Not even close.

What we haven't talked about yet—and what makes all the difference once you've learned to ground yourself—is what you *do* with the thoughts that show up alongside the panic. The catastrophic narratives. The worst-case scenarios. The absolute certainty that something terrible is happening or about to happen.

Because you can anchor yourself to the present moment all you want, but if your mind is still spinning disaster stories, you're only halfway there.

That's where we're going next.

A woman once showed me a tiny snow globe, the kind you'd find in a gas station gift shop, with a plastic palm tree inside.

The objects people carry aren't magical talismans; they are reminders of their own agency—a point of contact with the present moment when internal experience overwhelms them.

Chapter 7: Challenging Catastrophic Thoughts

I want you to finish this sentence: 'If my heart starts racing, it means...'

Whatever you just thought—hold onto it. We'll come back to it.

Whatever you just thought—hold onto it. We'll come back to it.

In 1997, a woman named Karen Overhill walked into Richard Baer's psychiatry office in Chicago complaining of severe headaches and blackouts. She was forty years old. Married. Worked in a hospital cafeteria. Seemed, on the surface, like someone dealing with stress and fatigue—nothing particularly unusual.

Over the course of treatment, Baer discovered she had seventeen distinct personalities, each with different handwriting, different memories, different ages. One was a frightened seven-year-old girl who drew pictures of houses with all the windows covered. Another was a hostile teenage boy who chain-smoked and spoke only in obscenities. Another was a nurturing middle-aged woman who had memorized lullabies in languages Karen didn't speak.

Dissociative identity disorder—what used to be called multiple personality disorder—remains one of the most contested diagnoses in psychiatry. Skeptics argue it's iatrogenic, created by suggestion during therapy. Believers point to brain imaging studies showing different neural patterns when different alters are present. The debates get heated, academic, bogged down in methodology.

But here's what nobody disputes: Karen's mind had learned to interpret certain triggers—a raised voice, a specific smell, a feeling of being trapped—as signals of such profound danger that her consciousness would fracture entirely rather than face the memory. Her father had abused her for years, starting when she was six. And somewhere along the way, her brain decided that the only way to survive those moments was to not be there at all. To become someone else. Anyone else.

That's an extreme example. The most extreme example, really—the outer edge of what a human mind will do to protect itself from perceived threat.

But the mechanism? The same one operating in your chest right now when your heart starts to race and your mind immediately supplies a story about what that racing means.

Your body isn't trying to kill you. But your thoughts about your body—the stories you tell yourself about what a racing heart or a wave of dizziness or a flutter in your chest *means*—might be slowly killing your life.

I'm thinking of David again. The accountant I mentioned earlier, the one who thought his body had turned traitor during a panic attack at the diner.

Between his first attack and the day we talked, he spent six months cataloging every heartbeat. Every breath. Every flutter, every twinge, every moment of lightheadedness. He bought a pulse oximeter—one of those little clip-on devices that measures oxygen saturation—and checked it seventeen times a day. Sometimes more if he was having what he called "a bad day."

He kept a spiral notebook where he logged the exact time and intensity of each symptom. The pages were covered in his cramped handwriting: "2:47 PM - heart rate elevated, 98 bpm, felt 'off'" "5:13 PM - brief dizziness, lasted ~10 seconds, no obvious trigger" "11:32 PM - palpitations while lying down, rate jumped to 105, took 8 minutes to return to baseline."

The notebook wasn't helping him track patterns so he could identify triggers and make productive changes. It was a record of his terror, translated into data points that felt more manageable than the raw fear underneath.

He wasn't cataloging symptoms. He was translating every bodily sensation into evidence of impending catastrophe.

Here's what that looked like in practice: A slight uptick in heart rate while climbing stairs—from seventy-five to ninety beats per minute, a completely normal cardiovascular response to exertion—became proof his system was failing. A moment of breathlessness after rushing to catch the train meant he was suffocating, that his lungs weren't working right, that something was terribly wrong. A flutter in his chest while lying in bed at night—probably a premature ventricular contraction, the kind most people experience daily without noticing because they're not monitoring every electrical impulse like it's a bomb countdown—became a sign that this was it, the big one, the heart attack that would kill him before he turned thirty-five.

The cost wasn't abstract.

David stopped playing pickup basketball on Thursday nights because running might trigger palpitations. He stopped drinking coffee—not just cutting back, but eliminating it entirely, even though he'd loved the ritual of his morning pour-over for years. He stopped eating spicy food because capsaicin raises body temperature and he'd convinced himself that any increase in heart rate, for any reason, was dangerous. He stopped doing anything that might make his heart beat faster than its resting rate.

He started sleeping with his phone on the nightstand, volume turned all the way up, the screen angled so he could see it without lifting his head, ready to call 911 the second his body betrayed him. He'd lie there in the dark, fingers pressed to his wrist, counting beats, calculating whether the rhythm was regular enough or if this was the night everything would finally give out.

His girlfriend left him.

Not because she didn't care. She did. She loved him, actually, which is why she tried for as long as she did. But she couldn't compete with the monitoring, the constant reassurance-seeking ("Does my pulse feel normal to you? Can you check?"), the nightly ritual of him lying perfectly still in bed, barely breathing, listening to his heart like it was a bomb that might go off.

"You're not here with me," she told him when she finally packed her things. "You're somewhere else. Inside your own head. Listening to your heart. And I can't reach you anymore."

She was right.

And the thing that kills me—the thing that still makes me angry when I think about it—is that David's heart was fine. Completely fine. He'd been to three cardiologists. He'd had an EKG, an echocardiogram, a stress test, a Holter monitor that recorded every beat for forty-eight hours straight. They all told him the same thing: structurally sound, electrically normal, no cause for concern.

But he didn't believe them. Because the catastrophic thought in his head—*my racing heart means I'm dying*—felt more real, more true, more certain than any test result.

Most people, when they describe this pattern to me, minimize it.

They say, "I'm managing." They say, "It's not that bad." As if acknowledging the full weight of what they've lost would make them weak or dramatic or ungrateful for the good things still left in their lives.

But I want to talk about what *managing* actually looks like. What it costs. Not in some vague, hand-wavy way, but in concrete terms—the life you used to have versus the life you're living now.

Sarah, the graphic designer I mentioned in Chapter 3, stopped going to her favorite coffee shop. The one on Seventh Avenue with the huge windows and the barista who knew her order before she opened her mouth. Oat milk latte, extra shot, no foam. She'd been going there three, four times a week for two years. She knew which table got the best light in the afternoon. She'd done some of her best work there, sketch pad open, watching people walk by.

Too crowded, she told herself after the panic attacks started. Too loud. The espresso machine hissing, people talking over each other, the scrape of chairs on the concrete floor—it all felt like too much input, too much stimulation, like her nervous system couldn't handle that much sensory information without short-circuiting.

She started getting her coffee from the place near her apartment instead. The one that felt sterile and fluorescent, where the barista never made eye contact and the coffee tasted like it had been sitting on the burner for three hours. But there were never more than three people in line. She could get in, get out, minimize her exposure to potential triggers.

Then she stopped meeting friends for dinner.

Restaurants made her nervous—the noise, the confined space, the inability to leave quickly if she needed to. What if she had a panic attack at the table? What if she couldn't breathe and everyone was staring and she couldn't get out because she was wedged into a booth against the wall?

She'd suggest takeout instead, eaten at someone's apartment where she could control the environment. Her friends went along with it at first. Then the invitations started coming less frequently. Then they stopped.

Then she started declining work projects that required client meetings.

She'd say she was swamped, that she couldn't take on anything new right now, that maybe next quarter when things calmed down. Her boss believed her for a while. He was understanding, even sympathetic—everyone gets overwhelmed sometimes, he said. Take the time you need.

Then he stopped offering.

Each concession felt small. Reasonable, even. It's not that big a deal to switch coffee shops. It's not the end of the world to skip a dinner out. It's responsible, actually, to turn down work you're not sure you can handle.

But stacked together? Sarah had built a cage around herself, one careful decision at a time, each bar forged from a story she told herself about what her anxiety meant. About what would happen if she didn't avoid the things that made her nervous.

And here's the part that probably sounds familiar: she told herself she was being smart. Proactive. Managing her anxiety responsibly instead of just pushing through and making it worse.

But there's a difference between accommodation and avoidance. Accommodation means adjusting the environment in a way that allows you to participate. Avoidance means shrinking your life to fit inside the boundaries of your fear.

Sarah was doing the latter. And it was costing her everything.

David did the same thing with presentations at work.

He started over-preparing—rehearsing his slides until two in the morning, memorizing every transition, writing out answers to every conceivable question and drilling them until his delivery sounded mechanical. He told himself this was professionalism. Diligence. The mark of someone who took their work seriously.

What it actually was: a desperate attempt to engineer certainty in a situation that couldn't be controlled.

Because the catastrophic thought running underneath all that preparation wasn't *I want to do a good job*. It was *if I make even one mistake, everyone will see how broken I am.*

The more he tried to prevent any possibility of stumbling—any pause, any um, any moment of not knowing the answer immediately—the more rigid he became. He'd stand at the front of the conference room, hands gripping the podium to hide the tremor, voice carefully modulated to mask the fear, and deliver his perfectly memorized script.

His colleagues started noticing.

"You seem tense," they'd say. "You okay, man?"

Which only amplified the fear. The fear of being judged, of his anxiety being visible, of everyone in the room seeing what he desperately wanted to hide.

So he'd prepare even harder for the next one. Stay up even later. Memorize even more. Try to control every variable, every possible point of failure.

And the presentations got worse. More wooden. More rehearsed. Less human.

This is what catastrophic thinking does. It doesn't just make you uncomfortable in the moment. It fundamentally reshapes how you move through the world. You start organizing your entire life around avoiding a feeling.

And the feeling you're avoiding? It's temporary. It's harmless. It's literally just your nervous system doing what nervous systems do when they perceive a threat—even a threat that doesn't exist.

Let me be clear about what's actually happening in your body after a panic attack. Not in vague, simplified terms, but the actual physiological sequence.

When your nervous system activates the fight-or-flight response, it releases stress hormones: adrenaline from your adrenal glands, cortisol from your hypothalamic-pituitary-adrenal axis. Your heart rate spikes—sometimes to 120, 140, even 180 beats per minute depending on how intensely your amygdala is screaming DANGER. Your breathing quickens and becomes shallow, shifting from diaphragmatic breathing to chest breathing. Blood flow redirects from your digestive system and your skin to your large muscle groups—your quads, your glutes, your lats—because if you're about to fight or run, those are the muscles that need oxygen. Your pupils dilate so you can take in more visual information. Your hands get cold because blood has moved away from your extremities toward your core. You might feel nauseated because your stomach has essentially paused digestion—why waste energy breaking down lunch when you might be someone else's lunch? You might feel dizzy because you're hyperventilating, blowing off too much CO2, and altering the pH balance in your blood.

All of this is your body preparing to either fight a predator or run from it.

If you were actually facing a mountain lion, this response would be perfect. Adaptive. Exactly what evolution designed it to do over millions of years of hominid development.

But that surge doesn't shut off the instant the perceived threat disappears.

Think about a car engine that's been redlined. You're driving down the highway, you floor it to pass a semi, the RPMs spike into the red zone, the engine is screaming—then you ease off the gas and merge back into your lane. The engine doesn't instantly cool down. The temperature gauge doesn't immediately drop back to normal. It takes time for the metal to stop expanding, for the oil to circulate and dissipate the heat, for the parts to stop vibrating at that intense frequency, for everything to return to baseline.

Your nervous system works the same way.

It revved up to handle a threat—even if that threat was illusory, even if it was just your mind misinterpreting a crowded grocery store or a work presentation or a random flutter in your chest as a life-or-death situation—and now it needs time to recalibrate. To metabolize the adrenaline. To bring cortisol levels back down. To shift blood flow back to your digestive system and your skin. To normalize your breathing pattern.

That process takes time. Twenty minutes, sometimes. Thirty. Occasionally longer if the activation was particularly intense.

And during that window—that perfectly normal, completely harmless recovery window—you're going to feel residual symptoms.

Your heart might still be beating faster than usual. Your hands might still be a little shaky. You might still feel a knot in your stomach or a tightness in your chest or a slight sense of unreality, like you're watching yourself from outside your body.

That heightened state isn't a sign another attack is imminent. It's not evidence that something is wrong with you. It's simply your system coming down from an activation that was, from your body's perspective, completely justified.

But here's where the catastrophizing starts.

You feel your heart still beating fast—maybe it's been twenty minutes since the panic peaked, but your pulse is still at ninety beats per minute instead of your normal seventy. And instead of recognizing this as the natural aftermath of a stress response, you interpret it as evidence that something is wrong. That another attack is building. That your body is spiraling out of control.

A racing heart becomes proof of impending doom.

Shallow breaths become confirmation that you're suffocating.

A slight tremor in your hands becomes a sign that you're losing your grip on reality.

And those interpretations—those stories you tell yourself about what the sensations mean—trigger a cascade of additional stress hormones. Which keep your nervous system stuck in high gear. Which produce more symptoms. Which you interpret as further evidence that catastrophe is imminent.

You're standing on the gas pedal even after you've reached your destination. You're amplifying the very sensations you're trying to escape.

And that amplification is fueled entirely by catastrophic thinking: those automatic, exaggerated interpretations that transform a normal physiological response into a sign of imminent disaster.

Maya fell into this trap completely.

After her panic attack at the grocery store—the one I described in Chapter 2, where she abandoned a full cart in the cereal aisle and sat in her car for forty minutes waiting for her hands to stop shaking—she started scanning her body constantly for any hint of discomfort.

Not consciously, at first. It started as a background process, like a virus scanner running on your computer, constantly checking, constantly monitoring.

A slight headache while reading before bed? Must be anxiety building.

A momentary wave of dizziness when she stood up too quickly—orthostatic hypotension, a completely normal drop in blood pressure that happens to everyone occasionally? Definitely the start of another attack.

A flutter in her chest while watching TV? Panic. Had to be panic.

She'd feel the sensation, and immediately—*immediately*, before she could even complete a conscious thought—her mind would supply the interpretation: *This is it. It's happening again. I need to do something right now or I'm going to lose control.*

This constant self-monitoring created a feedback loop.

The more she scanned for symptoms, the more symptoms she found. And here's why: the human body produces dozens of sensations every minute. Your heart skips a beat—benign premature atrial contractions that every healthy heart experiences. Your stomach gurgles because you're digesting food. You feel a twinge in your shoulder because you slept in a weird position. A tickle in your throat because the air is dry. A moment of lightheadedness when you turn your head too fast because the fluid in your inner ear took a second to catch up.

Most people don't notice these sensations because they're busy living their lives, their attention directed outward—toward work, toward conversation, toward the show they're watching or the book they're reading.

But when you're hypervigilant, when you're convinced that any unusual sensation might be the first domino in a cascade toward panic? You notice everything.

And you interpret everything as dangerous.

Maya started carrying Xanax in her purse, just in case. Her doctor had prescribed it for acute anxiety, to be taken as needed—half a milligram, no more than twice a day.

Then she started taking half a pill preemptively before going anywhere that made her nervous. The grocery store. The mall. A friend's birthday party.

Then she started taking a full pill instead of half.

Then two pills.

Then she started taking them at home, too, because what if anxiety hit her there and she wasn't prepared?

Her doctor warned her about tolerance. About dependence. About rebound anxiety—the phenomenon where benzodiazepines, when taken regularly, can actually create more anxiety than they relieve because your brain downregulates its own GABA receptors in response to the external supply of GABA agonists.

She nodded. She said she understood. She promised she'd cut back.

Then she went home and took another pill because her chest felt tight and she couldn't risk having another attack.

The catastrophic thought driving all of this: *If I feel anxious, I won't be able to handle it. I'll spiral completely. I need to stop it before it starts.*

But here's the problem with that thought. Actually, here are several problems with it.

First: Maya *had* handled anxiety before. Many times. She'd had panic attacks and survived them. They were terrifying, yes. Excruciating, absolutely. But she was still here. Still alive. Still functional. The anxiety hadn't destroyed her. It had been temporary—always temporary—even when it felt infinite in the moment.

Second: by medicating every hint of discomfort before it could fully develop, she was preventing herself from learning that she could tolerate distress. She was reinforcing the belief that anxiety was dangerous, that it required immediate intervention, that her own internal resources weren't sufficient to handle it.

Third: the Xanax wasn't solving the problem. It was masking it. And in the process, it was creating a new problem—dependence on a substance that was supposed to be a short-term tool, not a long-term crutch.

But she couldn't see any of that. Because the catastrophic thought had become gospel truth in her mind, and everything she did was in service of avoiding the disaster she was certain would happen if she didn't intervene.

Ben's catastrophic thinking took a different shape.

His wasn't about physical symptoms. It was about emotional collapse—the fear that if he allowed himself to fully feel his grief after his wife died, he would be overwhelmed and unable to cope. That the sadness would swallow him whole and he'd never find his way back out.

He interpreted sadness as weakness. Loneliness as proof that he was destined to be alone forever. Any moment of crying as evidence that he was falling apart, that he wasn't strong enough to handle what life had thrown at him.

So he shut it down. He stayed busy. He took extra shifts at work, volunteered to cover for colleagues, filled every empty hour with tasks and obligations and distractions so he wouldn't have to sit with the feeling.

But grief doesn't disappear because you ignore it.

It just builds pressure, like water behind a dam, until the smallest crack becomes a rupture.

For Ben, the crack came at the grocery store—not because the store itself was dangerous, but because it was the place where he and his wife used to shop together every Saturday morning. They had a whole routine. She'd handle produce and dairy, he'd get the meat and the canned goods, they'd meet in the middle and argue affectionately about which kind of pasta sauce to buy. She liked the one with the basil, he liked the one with the roasted garlic. They'd end up getting both.

Walking down that aisle eight months after she died, seeing the brand of crackers she loved, hearing a song over the speakers that they'd danced to in their kitchen one night after too much wine—all of it crashed into him at once.

And the dam broke.

He had a panic attack. Heart racing, vision tunneling, a crushing sensation in his chest that felt exactly like what he imagined a heart attack would feel like.

Not because his body was malfunctioning. But because he'd been catastrophizing grief, treating normal human sadness like a threat that needed to be contained.

The story he was telling himself: *If I let myself feel this, I'll never stop. I'll drown in it. I won't survive.*

But feelings don't work that way.

They're waves, not floods. They rise, they crest, they recede. Always. The only way to drown is to fight the wave—to thrash and panic and exhaust yourself trying to push it away instead of letting it move through you.

Ben didn't know that yet. So he fought. And the fighting turned grief into panic, turned a natural human response to loss into a medical emergency.

You might be thinking: *Okay, fine, but what if my thoughts are actually accurate? What if I'm not catastrophizing? What if something really is wrong?*

This is the question I get more than any other. And it's a fair question. Because the truth is, sometimes things *are* wrong.

Sometimes a racing heart is a sign of a cardiac issue. Sometimes dizziness is a symptom of something that needs medical attention. Sometimes the anxiety you're feeling is actually your body trying to tell you something important.

So let me be clear: I'm not suggesting you ignore symptoms. I'm not suggesting you dismiss every uncomfortable sensation as "just anxiety" and power through without ever seeking medical evaluation.

If you're experiencing new, unexplained symptoms—especially symptoms like chest pain, shortness of breath, unexplained weight loss, persistent dizziness, or anything else that feels genuinely different from your baseline—get it checked out. See a doctor. Get the tests. Rule out the scary stuff.

But here's the thing: most people dealing with panic attacks have *already done that*. They've been to the ER multiple times. They've had EKGs, blood work, imaging. They've been told, repeatedly, by multiple medical professionals, that there's nothing physically wrong.

And they still don't believe it.

Because the catastrophic thought doesn't operate on evidence. It operates on fear. And fear is a much more powerful motivator than logic.

So the question isn't "What if something is wrong?" The question is: "Have I already had this checked out? Have I been medically cleared? And if so, am I still seeking reassurance because I genuinely think the doctors missed something, or because I'm terrified and I want someone to make the feeling go away?"

If it's the latter—and for most people struggling with panic, it is—then seeking more reassurance, getting more tests, checking your pulse oximeter for the eighteenth time today isn't helping you. It's feeding the catastrophic thinking. It's reinforcing the belief that your body is dangerous and requires constant surveillance.

And that reinforcement is what keeps you stuck.

So how do you break this pattern?

First, you have to catch yourself in the act of catastrophizing.

This sounds simple. It's not. These thoughts happen so automatically, so quickly, with such complete conviction, that we barely notice them. They feel like observations, like facts, rather than interpretations. Your heart races, and the thought "I'm having a heart attack" arrives so instantly, with such certainty, that it doesn't register as a thought at all. It registers as truth.

The key is developing what cognitive therapists call metacognitive awareness—the ability to observe your own thinking process without getting swept up in it. To create enough distance that you can see the thought as an event in your mind rather than an accurate reflection of reality.

Here's how to start.

The next time you notice anxiety rising, pause. Don't try to fix it, don't try to make it go away, don't immediately reach for your phone to check your pulse or google your symptoms or text someone for reassurance. Just pause.

And ask yourself: *What am I telling myself right now?*

Not what you're feeling—you already know you're feeling anxious. But what story are you constructing about those feelings? What narrative is your mind offering up to explain the sensations in your body?

Write it down if you can. Say it out loud if you're alone. Get the thought out of your head and into the open where you can examine it.

For Amelia—the mom I mentioned in an earlier chapter, the one unloading groceries when her chest suddenly tightened—the thought was: *This tightness in my chest means I'm losing control and something terrible is about to happen.*

For Sarah: *If I go into that crowded coffee shop, I'll have another panic attack and everyone will think I'm crazy.*

For David: *If I make even one mistake during this presentation, my entire career will be over and everyone will see how incompetent I really am.*

For Ben: *If I let myself cry, I'll never be able to stop.*

These are catastrophic thoughts.

Not because they're necessarily irrational on their face—sometimes presentations do go badly, sometimes people do judge you, sometimes grief feels bottomless—but because of the certainty, the finality, the all-or-nothing quality of the prediction.

One mistake doesn't end a career. But in the grip of catastrophic thinking, it feels like it will.

Crying doesn't last forever. But when you're terrified of your own emotions, it feels like it might.

Once you've identified the catastrophic thought, the next step is to test it against reality.

Not in some abstract, theoretical way. Not by trying to logic yourself out of the feeling or convince yourself that you're being silly. With actual evidence from your own life.

Ask yourself: *Has this catastrophic prediction ever actually come true?*

When you've felt this way before—and you have felt this way before, probably dozens or hundreds of times—what actually happened?

Most of the time, the answer is: nothing.

Or at least, nothing remotely close to what you feared.

You felt terrible, yes. Uncomfortable, absolutely. Your heart raced, your palms sweated, your mind spun with worst-case scenarios, you were convinced you were dying or losing your mind or about to humiliate yourself in some irreversible way.

But you didn't die. You didn't lose your mind. You didn't collapse in public humiliation while everyone pointed and laughed. The catastrophe you predicted didn't materialize.

The anxiety was temporary. It peaked—sometimes after five minutes, sometimes after twenty, sometimes after an hour—it plateaued, and eventually—*always*—it passed.

This isn't just a mental exercise. It's retraining your brain to recognize patterns.

Because every time you catastrophize and nothing terrible happens, you're actually reinforcing the very fear you're trying to escape. You're teaching your brain that the only reason disaster didn't strike is because you avoided it, because you left the grocery store early, because you turned down the invitation, because you pulled over on the highway and waited for your heart to slow down.

Your brain draws a causal link: *I avoided disaster by escaping. Therefore, escaping kept me safe. Therefore, I must always escape to stay safe.*

But if you can start collecting evidence that anxiety itself is harmless—that it's uncomfortable but not dangerous, that it peaks and passes regardless of what you do—you begin to weaken that fear response.

You begin to separate the feeling from the story you've been telling about what the feeling means.

I learned this the hard way.

I don't talk about this much—not because it's a secret, but because I spent a long time thinking it disqualified me from helping other people. Like, who was I to guide someone through anxiety when I'd spent two years of my own life convinced I was dying?

I was twenty-six. In graduate school, working on my clinical hours, absolutely buried under the pressure of proving I belonged in a field where everyone else seemed smarter, more capable, more naturally suited to the work than I was.

And one night, lying in bed, I felt my heart skip.

Just once. A little flutter, a brief pause, then back to normal rhythm.

I noticed it. And the instant I noticed it, my mind supplied the interpretation: *Something's wrong.*

I felt it again an hour later. Then again the next morning. Then five times that afternoon.

I went to my doctor. Got an EKG. Normal. He said it was probably stress, probably benign PVCs—premature ventricular contractions—something most people experience without ever noticing. Told me to cut back on caffeine, get more sleep, maybe see a therapist about the anxiety I was clearly experiencing.

I didn't believe him.

I went to a cardiologist. Got a Holter monitor, wore it for forty-eight hours while it recorded every beat. The results came back: occasional PVCs, nothing concerning, normal variant for someone my age.

Still didn't believe it.

I started checking my pulse constantly. I'd be in a supervision meeting, fingers pressed to my wrist under the table, counting beats. I'd be driving, one hand on the wheel, the other on my chest, feeling for irregularities. I'd lie awake at night, utterly still, listening to my heart, waiting for the next skip.

And every time I felt one, the catastrophic thought would arrive: *This is it. This time it's the big one. This time it's not going to correct itself.*

It took me eighteen months to realize that the more attention I paid to my heart, the more I noticed. And the more I noticed, the more I panicked. And the more I panicked, the more adrenaline flooded my system. And adrenaline causes—guess what—ectopic heartbeats.

I was creating the very thing I was afraid of.

I only figured it out because I got so exhausted from the hypervigilance that I eventually just... gave up. Not in a dramatic way. I didn't have some breakthrough moment of clarity. I just got tired. Tired of monitoring. Tired of being afraid. Tired of living like my body was a ticking bomb.

So one day I decided: fine. If I'm going to die from a heart arrhythmia, I'm going to die while doing something more interesting than checking my pulse.

And I stopped checking.

I went for a run—something I'd been avoiding for months because what if exertion triggered a fatal arrhythmia? I drank coffee. I stayed up late working on a paper. I did all the things I'd been cataloging as dangerous.

And nothing happened.

My heart kept beating. Irregularly sometimes, yes, but it kept beating. The skipped beats didn't escalate into cardiac arrest. The catastrophe I'd been predicting for eighteen months never came.

What did happen: I got my life back. Slowly, piece by piece, as I accumulated evidence that the feeling I'd been catastrophizing was just a feeling. Uncomfortable, yes. Alarming, absolutely. But not dangerous.

That's what I mean when I say this isn't just theory. I've lived it. I know what it's like to be so convinced that your body is betraying you that you organize your entire existence around monitoring for signs of failure.

And I know what it's like on the other side—when you stop fighting the sensations and start questioning the story you've been telling yourself about what they mean.

I'm thinking of a patient I worked with a few years ago. I'll call her Rachel.

She'd developed such intense fear of having a panic attack while driving that she stopped using highways entirely. She'd take surface streets, even if it meant turning a twenty-minute commute into an hour-long ordeal through residential neighborhoods and stoplights and school zones where kids darted into the street chasing soccer balls.

Her husband thought she was being ridiculous. "Just get on the highway," he'd say, exasperated after she'd shown up late to yet another event because she'd taken the long way. "You're fine. Nothing's going to happen."

But he didn't understand. For Rachel, the highway wasn't just inconvenient or nerve-wracking. It was genuinely terrifying in a way that felt as real and immediate as if someone had put a gun to her head.

Her catastrophic thought: *If I panic while driving on the highway, I'll lose control of the car and cause a terrible accident. I'll kill myself or someone else.*

When we examined this thought together in our first session, I asked her: "Have you ever actually lost control of the car during a panic attack?"

She paused. Thought about it. "Well, no," she admitted. "But I've pulled over immediately. I white-knuckled it to the shoulder and stopped."

"Okay," I said. "So even in the middle of a panic attack—heart racing, hands shaking, feeling like you couldn't breathe—you were able to safely navigate the car to the shoulder and stop. You checked your mirrors, you signaled, you steered, you braked. That's not losing control. That's maintaining control under extremely difficult circumstances."

She looked at me like I'd just performed a magic trick. Like I'd reframed something she'd been certain of for so long that she'd never thought to question the underlying assumption.

I asked her what she thought would have happened if she hadn't pulled over. If she'd just kept driving, stayed in her lane, kept her hands on the wheel, and let the panic run its course without responding to it.

She looked at me like I'd suggested she juggle chainsaws while blindfolded.

"I would have crashed," she said with absolute certainty.

"Based on what?" I asked.

She didn't have an answer. Just a feeling. A bone-deep conviction that panic and control were mutually exclusive, that you couldn't experience one while maintaining the other.

So we tested it.

Not recklessly. Not all at once. We started with short highway drives during off-peak hours—Sunday morning at seven a.m. when traffic was light and the roads were mostly empty. Just one exit. Then two.

The first time she felt anxiety rising—her heart starting to speed up, her breathing getting shallow, that familiar tightness in her chest that signaled the beginning of a panic attack—she kept driving instead of pulling over.

And you know what happened?

Nothing.

She didn't crash. She didn't swerve into another lane. She didn't freeze up and forget how to steer. Her hands stayed on the wheel, her foot stayed on the gas, and she made it to her exit safely.

The anxiety was excruciating, she told me later. Her heart was pounding so hard she thought it might burst through her ribs. She was gripping the steering wheel so tight her knuckles went white. Every fiber of her being was screaming at her to pull over, to stop, to get out of the car and wait for the feeling to pass.

But she didn't. She kept driving.

And the catastrophe she'd been predicting for months—the loss of control, the crash, the disaster—didn't happen.

We repeated this process multiple times over several weeks. Gradually building up to more challenging scenarios—two-lane highways, then three-lane, then rush hour traffic, then longer distances.

Each time, the same pattern: anxiety would spike, she'd be convinced she was about to lose control, she'd keep driving anyway, and the catastrophe wouldn't materialize.

And slowly—very slowly—her brain started to learn a new pattern. Started to accumulate evidence that panic, while intensely uncomfortable, wasn't actually dangerous. That she could feel her heart racing and her hands shaking and her thoughts spiraling and still maintain control of the car.

The catastrophic thought began to lose its power. Not because she reasoned it away or convinced herself it was silly, but because she tested it in the real world and discovered it wasn't true.

Here's what I want you to understand: the goal isn't to eliminate panic.

I know that sounds counterintuitive. You picked up this book because you want the panic to stop. You want your body to feel normal again. You want to go back to the way things were before the first attack, when you didn't spend every moment monitoring your heartbeat or planning your escape routes or catastrophizing every flutter in your chest.

I get it. I wanted that too.

But trying to eliminate panic is what keeps you stuck. Because the more you fight it, the more you fear it, the more you organize your life around avoiding it—the stronger it becomes.

The goal isn't elimination. It's reframing. It's changing your relationship to the sensations so that they stop feeling like a five-alarm fire and start feeling like what they actually are: your body's overprotective security system misfiring.

A racing heart isn't a sign you're dying. It's a sign your sympathetic nervous system activated.

Shallow breathing isn't suffocation. It's a respiratory pattern that changes during stress.

Dizziness isn't a stroke. It's altered CO2 levels from hyperventilation.

These sensations are temporary. Always temporary. They peak, they plateau, they pass—usually within twenty to thirty minutes, sometimes faster if you stop fighting them and let them run their course.

But when you catastrophize—when you interpret a racing heart as a heart attack, when you treat dizziness like a medical emergency, when you convince yourself that this time the panic won't stop—you keep the stress response active. You keep standing on the gas pedal. You turn a temporary spike into a sustained activation.

The catastrophic thought is the thing that makes panic persistent.

Not your body. Not your nervous system. Your thoughts about what your body is doing.

So here's the homework. The real work. Not reading, not understanding—doing.

The next time you feel anxiety rising, I want you to name the catastrophic thought. Out loud if possible. Say it exactly as it appears in your mind: "I'm having a heart attack." "I'm going to pass out and everyone will see." "I'm losing my mind." "This feeling will never end."

Then ask yourself: "Is this true, or is this my fear talking?"

You don't have to believe the answer yet. You just have to ask the question.

Then—and this is the hard part—I want you to sit with the discomfort. Don't run. Don't distract. Don't check your pulse or google your symptoms or take a Xanax or call someone for reassurance.

Just sit. Breathe. Let the wave rise.

Notice where you feel it in your body. Notice the thoughts that accompany it. Notice the urge to escape, to fix, to make it stop.

And then notice that you're still here. Still breathing. Still conscious. Still in control, even though it doesn't feel like it.

The anxiety will pass. It always does.

And when it does, you'll have one more piece of evidence that the catastrophic thought was wrong. That the disaster you predicted didn't happen. That you survived.

You're collecting data. Building a new pattern. Teaching your brain that anxiety, while uncomfortable, is not dangerous.

That's how you break the cycle. Not by eliminating panic, but by changing what you believe panic means.

In the next chapter, we're going to talk about what comes after you stop running—how to gradually reclaim the parts of your life you've been avoiding, piece by piece, without retraumatizing yourself in the process. Because understanding that panic is temporary is one thing. Actually walking back into the situations that trigger it? That's where the real work begins.

If your heart starts racing and you immediately interpret it as dangerous, what other possibilities might you be overlooking? The next step is to test those assumptions.

Chapter 8: Building Confidence Through Exposure

I had my first panic attack in three years during a quarterly review presentation. Not at home, not in some anonymous public space where I could quietly slip away—in front of twelve colleagues and two senior directors, standing at a podium with a slide deck I'd rehearsed six times.

The grocery store looked exactly the same—same fluorescent lights, same cereal aisle, same cart handle cool under my palm. When my heart started pounding this time, I didn't run. Not because I wasn't afraid, but because I'd learned to recognize that first flicker of sensation – the prickle at the back of my neck – not as a threat, but as information.

Heart pounding first. Then the vision narrowing, like someone closing a curtain from the edges inward. My hands went cold. The familiar script: *This is it. You're going to faint. Everyone will see. You need to leave. Right now.*

Three years earlier, I would have excused myself. Mumbled something about feeling ill and fled. I would have spent the rest of the day replaying the humiliation, cataloging all the ways my body had betrayed me.

This time, I stayed.

Not out of courage. More like exhaustion with my own fear. I was tired of letting panic make my decisions. So I stood there, hands visibly shaking as I clicked to the next slide. My voice came out thinner than I wanted, but it came out. I made it through—not brilliantly, not the way I'd rehearsed it, but I made it through.

Here's what struck me afterward: nobody knew. Not one person in that room registered what had been happening inside me. A colleague even complimented my delivery on the way out. The catastrophe I'd been bracing for existed entirely in my own nervous system. The panic was real. The threat was not.

That realization changed everything.

Because the goal isn't to stop having panic attacks. It's to stop treating them like five-alarm fires when they're really just your body's overprotective security system misfiring.

Think about the last thing you turned down because you were afraid you might panic. Maybe it was a dinner invitation. A job interview. A road trip with friends.

You probably told yourself it was practical. *I'm just not ready yet. Maybe next time.* Reasonable-sounding justifications that protect you from immediate discomfort.

But here's what actually happened: you chose the smaller life.

You chose the version of yourself that fits inside the boundaries your anxiety has drawn. And every time you make that choice, the boundaries get a little tighter.

I mapped out my entire existence around avoidance for almost two years. Took surface streets instead of the freeway, adding thirty minutes to my commute. Stopped going to my favorite bookstore because it was in a busy mall. Declined evening plans because what if I had a panic attack and couldn't drive home? I needed an escape route, needed to know I could leave any situation instantly.

From the outside, my life looked mostly normal. I was still working, still functional. But I was living in an ever-shrinking radius of what felt safe.

And it worked. Sort of. I had fewer panic attacks. My anxiety stayed lower. I felt more in control.

But that control was a con. I wasn't managing my anxiety—I was negotiating with it, giving up pieces of my life in exchange for temporary relief. And anxiety is a terrible negotiator. Every concession I made just convinced my nervous system that yes, those situations *were* dangerous.

So the boundaries kept shrinking.

The friend who stopped inviting me out because I'd cancelled too many times. The project at work I passed on because it required travel. The relationship that never quite got off the ground because I couldn't explain why I needed to sit near the exit at every restaurant.

This is what avoidance actually costs. Not some hypothetical future regret. Your actual life, right now. The version of yourself you're not becoming because fear is making the decisions.

Maybe you're thinking: *That's easy for you to say now. But I'm not there yet. My panic is too intense. I'm not ready.*

I had that exact thought every time someone suggested I should "just face my fears."

But exposure therapy isn't about throwing yourself into your worst fear and hoping willpower carries you through. That's not treatment. That's torture.

What the research shows—and what I eventually learned—is that your nervous system changes through graduated, repeated exposure to manageable challenges. Not overwhelming ones. Manageable ones.

What it felt like, for me, was choosing to sit inside the burning house instead of running out. Knowing intellectually that the house isn't actually on fire doesn't make the heat any less convincing.

The paradox of recovery is this: the only way to prove to your nervous system that a situation is safe is to stay in it while it's screaming at you to leave. You can't logic your way out. You have to *experience* the thing—the racing heart, the tunnel vision, the overwhelming certainty that something terrible is about to happen—and then experience what comes after.

Which is usually just normalcy.

The meeting continues. The grocery store stays standing. You don't faint, don't die, don't implode.

Your body learns through repetition, not reasoning.

So how do you actually do this without just white-knuckling your way through terror?

You start small. Sometimes absurdly small.

Gradual exposure means building a ladder of feared situations, starting from the bottom rung—the thing that makes you anxious but not panicked—and working your way up incrementally.

After my first panic attack, I avoided grocery stores for months. Just the thought of walking into a Safeway made my pulse spike. So I ordered everything online.

When I finally decided to tackle this, I didn't start by doing a full shop on a Saturday afternoon. I started by driving to the store parking lot. I sat in my car, engine off, looking at the building. Felt the anxiety rise. And I stayed for five minutes.

Five minutes of sitting in a parked car. That was the whole exposure.

It felt ridiculous. It also felt surprisingly hard. But the point wasn't to feel comfortable. The point was to stay present with discomfort until my nervous system started to settle. That habituation only happens when you remain in the situation long enough for your body to realize no actual threat is materializing.

The next week, I walked to the entrance. Didn't go inside. Just stood near the automatic doors.

Week three: walked inside, grabbed a basket, walked to produce, and walked out.

Week four: bought bananas. One item.

Each step built on the previous one, adding just slightly more challenge. Some weeks I stayed at the same level. Some weeks I slid backward—anxiety spiked, I left too quickly, felt like I'd failed.

But failure is the wrong frame. This isn't a test you pass or fail. It's a training process. Your nervous system is learning a new response, and learning is messy.

Let me tell you about Sarah, because her story illustrates how exposure hierarchies work when the fear has stolen something central to your independence.

Sarah had her first panic attack while driving on Interstate 5, merging into rush-hour traffic near Seattle. Heart hammering, vision graying out, convinced she was having a heart attack. She pulled over, called 911. Paramedics arrived, ran an EKG. Physically fine. Psychologically shattered.

She stopped driving that day. Not just on highways—all driving.

For someone living in a city with mediocre public transit, this rewired her entire existence. She couldn't visit her sister in Tacoma. Couldn't get to her favorite hiking trails. Started turning down job opportunities if the commute looked complicated.

When we first mapped out her exposure hierarchy, she wanted to jump straight to highway driving. "That's the thing I need to fix. Let's just do it."

I understood the impulse. When something has taken that much from you, you want to reclaim it immediately.

But exposure therapy isn't about confronting your biggest fear in one dramatic showdown. It's about building a foundation of competence, brick by brick.

So we started with something that felt embarrassingly simple: sitting in her parked car in the driveway.

Just sitting. Keys in hand, not in the ignition.

She sat there for ten minutes the first day, feeling her heart rate rise. She practiced diaphragmatic breathing, extending the exhale. Didn't try to force the anxiety away. Just stayed with it.

Next step: turning the car on. Letting it idle. Not going anywhere.

Then: driving around the block at 9 PM, when the streets were empty.

Then: one mile on residential roads during off-peak hours.

Then: three miles during light traffic.

Each step was calibrated to produce manageable anxiety, not terror. And each time she completed a step without fleeing, her nervous system registered: *I did the thing. I felt afraid. Nothing bad happened.*

The setbacks mattered as much as the successes.

One afternoon, while practicing on a quiet residential street, a truck suddenly honked at her—she'd drifted slightly over the center line. The sound jolted her into immediate panic. She pulled over, hands shaking, crying, furious at herself. Called me convinced she'd undone all her progress.

But that moment wasn't a failure. It was information.

It showed her that unexpected stimuli could still trigger her panic response, and that she needed more practice tolerating surprise. So we adjusted her hierarchy. Added a step where she practiced with a friend in the passenger seat who would occasionally make sudden noises or ask startling questions.

It took her four months to get comfortable on the highway. Four months of incremental steps, repeated exposures, occasional backsliding.

But when she finally merged onto I-5 during moderate traffic and drove ten miles without pulling over, the look on her face—I wish I could describe it. Not triumph, exactly. More like quiet reclamation.

She texted me later that night: *I drove to Tacoma. Had dinner with my sister. Just got home.*

That was it. No exclamation points, no celebration. Just the simple fact of having done a completely ordinary thing that, for four months, had been impossible.

Here's what makes exposure therapy work: your brain is constantly running predictions, trying to anticipate what's about to happen based on past experience. If you've had a panic attack in a specific context—driving, grocery stores, crowded elevators—your brain files that context under "DANGER." Next time you encounter it, your amygdala fires up the alarm before anything bad actually happens.

This is anticipatory anxiety. Your nervous system preparing for a threat that exists only in memory.

The only way to update that prediction model is to create new experiences that contradict it. You have to show your brain, repeatedly, that the feared situation can occur without catastrophe. That you can feel anxious in a grocery store and leave with bananas, not in an ambulance.

This is called inhibitory learning. You're not erasing the old fear memory—you're building a new, competing memory that says: "Actually, this situation is safe." Over time, with enough repetition, the new memory becomes stronger. The fear response weakens.

But this only happens if you stay in the situation long enough for your anxiety to peak and then start to decline.

If you leave at the peak, when your panic is highest, you reinforce the old pattern. Your brain learns: "See? We *had* to escape. It was dangerous."

This is why avoidance feels so good in the moment and costs you so much in the long run. Every time you dodge a feared situation, you get immediate relief. Your anxiety drops. Feels like you made the right call.

But you've just taught your nervous system that avoidance is necessary for survival.

Staying is harder. Staying feels counterintuitive, sometimes even cruel.

Because distress and danger are not the same thing. Discomfort is not damage.

And your body can only learn the difference through direct experience.

Let me be honest about what this process actually feels like when you're in the middle of it.

It feels like you're doing it wrong.

Like you're pushing too hard or not hard enough. Like everyone else would handle this better, faster, with more grace.

There's a particular loneliness that comes with exposure work. Because from the outside, your challenges look trivial. "You're anxious about buying groceries? Walking into a store?" People who haven't experienced panic don't understand why these ordinary tasks feel so loaded.

So you do the work quietly. You practice your exposures alone, where nobody can see you sitting in a parked car breathing through waves of irrational fear. You celebrate victories that would seem meaningless to anyone else: *I stayed in the grocery store for twenty minutes today. I answered a phone call without checking the caller ID. I drove on the highway for three exits.*

These aren't small things.

But they require a kind of internal validation that can be hard to sustain. You have to believe that this slow, unglamorous work is worthwhile even when it feels like you're making no progress.

Setbacks are part of the process, not evidence that the process isn't working. Your nervous system isn't a linear progression chart. It's a biological system trying to recalibrate itself, and recalibration is messy. Some days will feel harder than others. That's normal. That's not failure.

The goal isn't to eliminate anxiety. It's to change your relationship with it—to move from a place where anxiety dictates your choices to a place where you can feel afraid and act anyway.

One thing I've noticed: there's a temptation to rely on what therapists call "safety behaviors." These are the small things you do to make a feared situation feel more tolerable.

Carrying a water bottle in case you need to calm down. Wearing sunglasses so people can't see your eyes. Keeping your phone in your hand. Having a friend on standby. Checking where the exits are. Bringing medication you might not even need but want close just in case.

These behaviors feel helpful. They reduce your anxiety in the moment. But they also subtly reinforce the idea that the situation *is* dangerous and that you need these protective measures to survive it.

The tricky part is that some of these behaviors—deep breathing, grounding techniques—are genuinely useful regulation tools. The difference is in how you use them. Are you using them as a bridge to staying present, or as a way to avoid feeling your anxiety fully?

I carried a water bottle with me everywhere for the first year after my initial panic attack. Rationally, I knew hydration wasn't preventing panic. But holding that bottle gave me a sense of control. Eventually, I had to wean myself off it. Not because there's anything wrong with carrying water—obviously that's fine—but because *I* needed to prove to myself that I could handle anxiety without clutching something for comfort.

That was surprisingly hard. Harder than some of the actual exposures.

Because it meant sitting fully in my discomfort without any props, without any escape hatches. Just me and my racing heart and the terrifying ordinariness of a Tuesday afternoon.

But that's where the real learning happens. When you strip away the safety behaviors and discover that you're still okay. That the panic is uncomfortable but not dangerous. That you can tolerate sensations you thought would destroy you.

Let me tell you what happened after that presentation—the one where I stayed at the podium despite the full-body panic.

I went back to my desk afterward, still shaky, and sat there for twenty minutes just breathing. Trying to process what had just happened. Part of me was waiting f

The grocery store wasn't just a location; it was a testing ground—an opportunity to apply learned skills in the face of discomfort, proving that action can rewrite ingrained patterns.

Chapter 9: Beyond Regulation

The presentation ended. I gathered my notes, walked back to my desk, and sat down. My hands were still shaking—not the slight tremor you can hide by folding your arms, but a full visible shake that made picking up my coffee cup feel like a dexterity test.

My hands were still shaking—not the slight tremor you can hide by folding your arms, but a full visible shake that made picking up my coffee cup feel like a dexterity test. It wasn't about eliminating the shaking entirely, though; it was about being able to acknowledge it, and then return my attention to the task at hand – noticing the chipped ceramic of my mug, seeing the plastic palm tree on a colleague's desk.

Three years. That's how long it had been since my last panic attack. Three years of teaching clients exactly these skills, of writing and speaking about nervous system regulation, of genuinely believing I'd graduated past this particular circle of hell. And there I was, standing at a podium in front of forty colleagues and senior executives, gripping a clicker with sweaty palms while my throat constricted and my vision tunneled to a pinpoint and every alarm in my body screamed *get out get out get out*.

I know what the old version of me would have done. The pre-treatment version, before I understood any of this. I would have made some excuse mid-presentation—feeling sick, needed water, technical difficulty—and fled to the nearest bathroom to ride it out in a locked stall. Would have called in sick the next day. Probably the day after that too. Would have started constructing elaborate avoidance strategies around future presentations until the category itself became forbidden territory, another sector of my professional life surrendered to fear.

But I stayed. Not because the panic suddenly evaporated once I applied the right technique. Not because I breathed my way into some zen state of calm. And definitely not because I'm particularly courageous—I don't want to romanticize this.

I stayed because underneath all that noise, underneath the racing heart and the tunnel vision and the screaming certainty that something was catastrophically wrong, a different knowing had taken root: *this cannot actually hurt me*.

I lost my place twice during the presentation. Had to pause, visibly flustered, and find my slide again while forty pairs of eyes watched me fumble. My voice cracked on the third slide—genuinely cracked, like I was thirteen again—and I had to clear my throat and start the sentence over. When I clicked to advance the PowerPoint, my hand shook so badly I dropped the remote. It clattered against the floor. I had to bend down and pick it up while my face burned.

The panic didn't care that I understood the physiology. Didn't care that I could label what was happening as "sympathetic nervous system activation" or "hyperventilation syndrome" or any other clinical term that might create intellectual distance. In that moment, with forty people watching, my body was convinced I was dying.

Here's what changed everything: when the presentation ended and people came up with questions, with comments, with follow-up thoughts they wanted to share, not a single person mentioned it. No one pulled me aside to ask if I was okay. No one looked concerned or alarmed or like they'd just witnessed someone barely holding it together. The catastrophe that felt like a five-alarm fire inside my nervous system had been completely, utterly invisible to everyone else in that room.

That gap—the chasm between how intense the panic felt internally and the total absence of external evidence that anything was wrong—didn't make the experience less real. My hands kept shaking for another twenty minutes after I sat down. I felt wrung out for the rest of the day, that particular exhaustion that comes after your body has been flooded with adrenaline it didn't actually need.

But it fundamentally shifted my relationship to those sensations. They were information. A misfiring alarm. An overprotective security system responding to a threat that didn't exist.

Not a verdict on my competence. Not proof I was broken. Not a sign I needed to restructure my entire career around avoiding public speaking.

Just... loud. And temporary. And survivable.

Which brings us to the question this entire book has been building toward: what do you actually *do* with all these skills once you've learned them? Once you can recognize a panic attack for what it is, once you've practiced grounding techniques until they're second nature, once you've done enough interoceptive exposure that a racing heart doesn't automatically mean catastrophe—what then?

Sarah sat across from me in my office one Tuesday afternoon, hands clasped so tightly in her lap that her knuckles had gone white. She's in her early forties, works in project management at a mid-sized tech company, the kind of competent professional who runs complex launches and manages teams and makes everything look effortless from the outside. She'd spent three months diligently practicing every technique we'd covered after a brutal series of panic attacks during a product launch left her unable to sleep through the night or make it through a team meeting without excusing herself.

Box breathing—she could do it in her sleep. Grounding exercises—she had the 5-4-3-2-1 sensory inventory memorized. Interoceptive exposure—she'd gotten to the point where she could deliberately trigger a racing heart by running in place and then sit with the sensation without dissolving into full-blown terror.

"It works," she told me. I could hear both genuine relief and deep frustration threaded through those two words. "When I'm actively doing the techniques, I can bring myself back. I can interrupt the spiral before it gets too bad."

She paused. Looked out the window at the parking lot below. Looked back at me.

"But then it's just... waiting. Like I'm holding a dam against an ocean. Like the panic is always right there on the other side and I'm just—constantly vigilant. Constantly managing."

She wasn't wrong about what she'd accomplished. She'd gotten remarkably skilled at crisis management, at putting out fires the moment they started to catch. That's not nothing. Those skills matter. But they existed in isolation, tools she pulled out only *when* things started to feel bad, only *when* her nervous system kicked into high alert.

And that approach has a ceiling. You can become extremely proficient at interrupting panic without ever addressing the underlying architecture of how you move through the world—the baseline relationship you have with your own body, the way you interpret its signals, the stories you tell yourself about what those signals mean.

Here's what that pattern actually costs you. Not in some abstract future-tense way, but concretely, in the texture of your daily life.

You wake up and the first thing you do—before you think about your day or what you want for breakfast or the conversation you're looking forward to having—is scan your body for evidence of activation. Racing heart? Tight chest? Shallow breathing? You run through a mental checklist of your coping skills like you're gearing up for battle before you've even gotten out of bed.

At work, you're only half-present in meetings because some part of your attention is always monitoring your internal state. *Is my heart racing? Do I feel dizzy? Is my breathing getting shallow? Can I make it through this without having to leave?* You might excel at your job—Sarah did—but you've forgotten what it feels like to just be fully engaged in the conversation happening in front of you, without one eye perpetually on the emergency exit.

You turn down invitations. Not every single one, but more than you'd like. Not because you don't want to see your friends or go to that concert or show up for your niece's birthday party, but because you're exhausted. Every social event requires a full risk assessment before you commit: How far is it from home? Will I be able to leave early if I need to? What's my escape route? Is there parking nearby so I don't have to take public transit? Will there be alcohol, and if so, will people notice if I don't drink because alcohol sometimes triggers palpitations?

You start keeping emergency medication in every purse, every jacket pocket, every drawer in your house. Just in case. You probably haven't needed to take it in months, but the idea of being somewhere without it feels impossible.

You build a life around anxiety management. And somewhere along the way—so gradually you don't even notice it happening—the management becomes the point. You forget that these techniques were supposed to be tools *toward* something larger, not the destination themselves. You're surviving. Functional. Getting through your days.

But you're not living. Not really. Not in the way you did before panic taught you to be afraid of your own heartbeat.

Sarah described it once as living in a house where the roof constantly leaks. She'd gotten very, very good at emergency maintenance—at running around with buckets and tarps and sealant whenever water started dripping through the ceiling. Could patch a hole in under three minutes. Kept supplies ready in every room. But she wasn't actually *living* in the house. Wasn't hosting dinners or painting the walls her favorite color or hanging art or any of the things you do when a house is a home instead of a construction site in permanent crisis mode.

What she needed—what most people need when they reach this stage—wasn't more techniques. Wasn't a more comprehensive toolkit or a better emergency protocol.

What she needed was integration.

Think about someone learning to drive. I did this with my daughter last year, spent six months in the passenger seat while she white-knuckled the steering wheel and obsessively monitored every mirror and checkbox on the list we'd made. Check mirrors. Signal. Adjust speed. Check blind spot. Check mirrors again. Monitor distance to the car ahead. It was exhausting just watching her, this total cognitive overload consumed by the sheer mechanics of not crashing.

Then one day—maybe three months in?—I realized she was telling me a story while driving. Actually telling me a story, with inflection and hand gestures (okay, one hand), not robotically reciting the steps of merging onto the highway. The mechanics had become automatic enough that she could drive and have a conversation at the same time. Could drive and think about something other than the immediate task of operating the vehicle.

Not because driving had become easy or risk-free. She was still a new driver on actual roads with actual traffic. But her nervous system had integrated the skills to the point where they didn't require her complete conscious attention anymore. The vigilance became background hum instead of screaming alarm.

That's the shift we're talking about with body awareness. Moving from active crisis intervention—where you're only paying attention when something feels wrong—to integrated baseline awareness, where noticing your body's signals becomes woven into the fabric of daily life. Not something you have to remember to do when you're spiraling. Not a technique you pull out in emergencies. Just... part of how you move through the world.

There's actual physiology behind this, and I'm going to share it because I think it matters, but I promise not to drown you in neuroscience jargon. Sustained practice of these techniques—mindful breathing, grounding, interoceptive exposure—cultivates what's called vagal tone. That's the strength and flexibility of the vagus nerve, the major communication highway between your brainstem and key organs like your heart and digestive system.

When you have better vagal tone, your nervous system isn't constantly scanning the environment for threats, primed to launch into fight-or-flight at the slightest provocation. It creates what researchers call a "wider window of tolerance"—the range of activation your body can experience before it tips into dysregulation.

Not immunity to anxiety. That's not the goal and never will be. But greater flexibility in how you respond when your nervous system does activate.

Cognitively, integration does something even more valuable: it creates space between stimulus and response. Viktor Frankl wrote about this decades ago, that gap where freedom lives. When your heart rate increases, you're not immediately swept into catastrophic thoughts about heart attacks or losing control. You notice the sensation *as* a sensation—just data your body is providing—and observe the thought *as* a thought before reacting to it.

That split-second of awareness is where everything changes. It's the difference between "my heart is racing, which means I'm having a panic attack, which means I need to leave immediately" and "my heart is racing. That's interesting. I wonder what's activating my system right now."

Same sensation. Completely different outcome.

For Sarah, integration started small. Almost absurdly small. We decided she'd do a three-minute body scan during her commute to work—not as an anxiety-reduction exercise, not to fix anything or make herself feel calmer, but just as a check-in. Notice the pressure of her back against the car seat. The temperature of the steering wheel under her hands. The sensation of her feet resting on the floor, the slight engagement of muscles when she pressed the gas or brake.

She hated it at first. Told me straight-out it felt pointless, almost insulting. She was still sitting in rush-hour traffic. Still running through the same mental to-do list of everything waiting for her at the office. She wanted techniques that *did* something, that actively fought back against the anxiety, not this passive noticing that seemed to accomplish nothing.

"What's the point?" she asked me during our fourth session, genuinely exasperated. "I sit there noticing my body and then I get to work and it's the same stress, the same meetings, the same anxiety."

I told her what I'm telling you: the less you're fighting, the less there is to fight against.

The paradox at the heart of this work is that the harder you try to force your body into a state of calm, the more you're sending the message that something is wrong—that you're not safe, that you need to be different than you are right now. And your nervous system, which is trying to protect you, hears that message loud and clear. Stays on high alert. Keeps the alarms ready.

But when you simply notice—when you observe your body's state without immediately trying to change it—you're sending a different message. *This is information. Not a crisis. I can be here with this.*

Sarah kept doing the body scans, mostly because she'd committed to trying and didn't want to quit. Six weeks in, she realized she'd slept through the night three times that week. Not perfectly—she still woke sometimes at 3 a.m. with her pulse already climbing—but when she woke, she didn't spend the next three hours lying rigid in bed, catastrophizing about the panic attack she was sure was coming.

Two months in, she caught herself laughing—really laughing—at something a colleague said during a team meeting. And here's what stopped her: she noticed the laughter, noticed her heart rate had elevated slightly in response to the amusement, and realized she'd made it through the entire observation without checking whether the elevated heart rate meant something was wrong.

The anxiety was just... there. Background noise. Not the main event.

Small shifts. Boring, incremental progress that doesn't make for inspiring before-and-after transformation stories. But cumulative. Building day by day into a different baseline relationship with her own body.

David came to therapy with a different kind of resistance. He's a retired high school English teacher—the kind who genuinely loved the job, who quotes Whitman at dinner parties and still gets worked up about the importance of teaching kids to read critically. Sharp. Articulate. The sort of person who apologizes for "rambling" and then delivers a perfectly structured three-point argument without notes.

He'd spent three years avoiding social gatherings after a panic attack during a parent-teacher conference left him convinced he was dying in front of a room full of increasingly concerned parents. Ended up in the ER that night. They ran tests, found nothing wrong with his heart, sent him home with a referral to a therapist and a printout about anxiety that he'd read once and then shoved in a drawer.

He wasn't afraid of people, he told me carefully. Wasn't developing agoraphobia or social phobia or whatever diagnostic box I might try to fit him into. He missed connection, missed the texture of conversations that ranged beyond weather and traffic. But he dreaded—and this is the word he used, *dreaded*—the possibility of becoming overwhelmed by sensory input in a crowded room. Too many voices layering over each other. Too much movement in his peripheral vision. That telltale tightness starting in his chest while he was surrounded by family members who would inevitably notice something was off and ask if he was okay, which would only make it worse.

So he'd started declining invitations. At first just the big ones—Thanksgiving, Christmas, his daughter's fortieth birthday party. Too overwhelming, too much stimulation, too risky. Then smaller gatherings started feeling fraught. Sunday dinners at his son's house. His grandson's soccer games. Eventually he was turning down coffee with old colleagues, one-on-one invitations that should have felt completely safe.

Each individual avoidance made sense. He wasn't being dramatic. He wasn't exaggerating the discomfort. He was protecting himself from something very real and very visceral. But the aggregate cost—the total weight of all those individual reasonable decisions—was a life increasingly lived in isolation. He was watching family milestones through photos his daughter texted him instead of being present for them. Was hearing about his grandson's goals secondhand instead of cheering from the sidelines.

We worked on incorporating interoceptive exposure into his daily walks. David already walked every morning—had for years—so we weren't adding a new habit. Just shifting the quality of attention during something he was already doing.

Not deliberately triggering intense discomfort. Not trying to recreate panic. Just paying attention to naturally occurring sensations that his body was already producing. The slight increase in heart rate when the path turned uphill. The way his breathing deepened to match the increased demand. The coolness of morning air against his face, particularly sharp on the days when it was cold enough that his skin felt almost raw. The subtle tension that appeared in his shoulders when he picked up his pace, the slight burn in his calves on the steeper sections of his route.

He hated it.

"I want to feel *better*," he told me after the second week, genuinely frustrated. "Not spend all this time cataloging what feels *bad*."

But that was the misunderstanding we needed to clear up. We weren't cataloging bad sensations, wasn't building some comprehensive inventory of discomfort. We were building sensory tolerance—expanding his window of what felt manageable, what his body could experience without his threat-detection system immediately flagging it as danger.

Panic attacks don't come out of nowhere. They feel like they do—that's part of what makes them so terrifying—but they're usually the culmination of smaller sensations that your nervous system has learned to interpret as threats. Elevated heart rate. Slight breathlessness. A flutter of adrenaline.

When you consistently avoid those sensations or immediately try to shut them down the moment they appear, you're teaching your nervous system that they *are* dangerous. That they require an emergency response. The window of tolerance gets narrower and narrower until eventually a slightly elevated heart rate from climbing stairs becomes indistinguishable from the beginning of a panic attack.

But when you practice noticing those sensations in contexts that are genuinely safe—on a morning walk, alone, no performance pressure, no audience—they start to lose their power to automatically escalate. Your nervous system learns: *Oh, this is just what happens when I walk uphill. This is normal activation, not danger.*

David committed to four weeks. Told me upfront he was skeptical but he'd try it, mostly because his daughter had asked him point-blank why he wasn't coming to family events anymore and he hadn't been able to give her an answer that didn't sound like he just didn't care.

The breakthrough came four months in. His grandson's eighth birthday party. First family gathering David hadn't found a reason to skip in eighteen months.

He called me two days later, and I could hear something different in his voice even before he started talking. Not quite excitement—David's too measured for that—but something looser. Less guarded.

His heart *did* race when the room got loud, when all the kids started shouting over the birthday cake and his son turned up the music and conversations were happening in overlapping layers all around him. His shoulders *did* tense. That familiar pressure started building in his chest, the one that used to feel like the opening notes of catastrophe.

But instead of interpreting those sensations as proof he needed to leave *right now*, as evidence that he was heading toward a panic attack and had to extract himself before it got worse—he recognized them.

Just his body responding to stimulation. Information about his nervous system's activation level. Not a directive. Not a command he had to obey.

He stayed for the whole party. Two and a half hours. He was honest with me that it wasn't comfortable. Didn't magically become easy once he reframed his interpretation. He felt activated and overstimulated and honestly kind of exhausted by the end.

But he stayed. And his grandson got to blow out the candles with his grandfather standing right there singing off-key with everyone else. And that mattered more than comfort.

This is where the work gets trickier, though. More nuanced. Less formulaic. Because life doesn't always present clean problems where the answer is just "practice more grounding techniques and gradually expose yourself to the thing you're avoiding."

What about when the source of anxiety isn't a specific situation you can desensitize to, but something deeply tangled with your values, your identity, your sense of who you're supposed to be and what your life is supposed to look like?

Leo sat in my office with his guitar case leaning against the wall—he'd come straight from teaching a lesson, still had a student's chord chart sticking out of his bag. He's a musician. Or he was. Or he is? The question itself was the source of the anxiety that had brought him to therapy.

He's in his mid-thirties now, and like a lot of musicians his age, he'd reached the point where the romanticized vision of making it as a performer had collided pretty hard with the reality of bills and health insurance and the fact that teaching music to middle schoolers paid significantly better than the gigs he could actually book. So teaching had become the compromise. The sensible choice. The thing that paid rent and gave him weekends and meant he didn't have to tour in a van sleeping on couches.

But lately—and by lately he meant the last three years—he'd been wrestling with a question that wouldn't let him sleep: should he quit his stable teaching job and actually try to make it as a performer? Go all-in on the thing he'd always said he wanted?

The anxiety around this decision was different from panic. Not acute. Not the kind of thing he could breathe through and watch dissolve. It was a constant low hum, a tightness that lived in his chest and flared whenever he let himself think seriously about the choice in front of him. He'd wake up at 2 a.m. and his mind would immediately start spinning through worst-case scenarios and best-case fantasies and everything in between until he felt like he was drowning in the sheer weight of the decision.

We started by slowing way down and actually exploring the physical sensations that accompanied each option. When Leo imagined quitting his job to pursue music full-time, what did his body do?

He closed his eyes. Sat quiet for a moment. "My chest gets tight," he said. "My stomach kind of... churns. Like I'm anxious."

He'd interpreted this as fear. As his body warning him away from danger, telling him the risk was too great, that he *shouldn't* make the leap. Evidence that the safe choice was the right choice.

But we kept going. I asked him to close his eyes again and actually pay attention to the sensations without immediately assigning meaning to them. Not "I feel anxious" but: what does the tightness actually feel like? Sharp or dull? Where exactly is it located? Does it change when you breathe into it? Is there anything else happening in your body alongside the tightness?

He sat quiet for what felt like a long time. I watched his breathing shift, deepen slightly. His face changed—some tension I hadn't even noticed releasing around his eyes.

When he opened them, he looked genuinely surprised.

"It's not just fear," he said slowly, like he was working it out as he spoke. "There's—I don't know how to describe it. Like energy? Excitement? It feels complicated. Like this... knot."

Exactly. Because anxiety about meaningful choices is rarely pure dread. It's almost always a complex tangle—uncertainty and hope and risk and possibility all wound together so tightly you can't tell where one ends and another begins. And when you lump all those sensations under the single label of "anxiety" and treat them as a unified warning signal telling you to back away from danger, you're cutting yourself off from valuable information.

We spent the next several sessions exploring how different parts of his body responded when he pictured each path forward. Teaching: a subtle collapse in his posture, like his whole body was settling into something resigned. A heaviness in his limbs. His breathing stayed shallow, didn't deepen or quicken, just stayed this constant surface-level rhythm that felt—he said this, not me—*gray*.

Performing: his shoulders lifted slightly, almost imperceptibly. His breathing deepened on its own. A warmth spread through his chest that felt adjacent to the tightness but not the same. And yes, also that churning in his stomach, that flutter of what could be fear or could be adrenaline or could be both.

This isn't magical thinking. I'm not suggesting your body has access to some mystical wisdom that your rational mind doesn't. It's simpler than that: your body is responding to these scenarios in real time based on your values, your desires, your sense of what matters. Those responses carry information.

Not directives. Your nervous system doesn't get to *make* the decision for you. A racing heart doesn't mean "do this thing" any more than a tight chest means "avoid this thing." But they're data points—one source of information alongside your intellectual reasoning, your practical considerations, your assessment of risk and reward.

Leo didn't walk out of our sessions with a clear answer handed to him by his nervous system. He ended up negotiating a one-year sabbatical from teaching to test the music path before committing fully, which honored both the excitement and the fear his body was signaling. Gave him a chance to actually find out what happened when he pursued the thing that made his breathing deepen and his shoulders lift, while also keeping a door open to return if it turned out the reality didn't match the hope.

The anxiety didn't disappear when he made the decision. He still wakes up sometimes at 2 a.m. wondering if he's making a massive mistake. But he stopped treating his body's responses as purely threat-detection and started treating them as one voice in a larger conversation about what kind of life he actually wanted to build.

Here's what would have happened if Leo had kept interpreting his anxiety as a simple warning system telling him to stay safe: he'd still be teaching, still feeling that gray heaviness in his limbs every morning when his alarm went off, still lying awake wondering if he'd missed his window. The anxiety about making the wrong choice would have calcified into the quieter, harder-to-name despair of never having chosen at all. Of getting to fifty and realizing he'd spent twenty years protecting himself from the risk of trying.

You might be thinking—and this is a thought Sarah voiced almost verbatim during one of our sessions—*This all sounds great in theory, but I'm three months into practicing these skills and I still wake up sometimes with my heart racing for absolutely no reason I can identify. Shouldn't I be better by now? Shouldn't this be working?*

Maya felt this acutely. She's in her early thirties, works in marketing for a tech startup where "fast-paced environment" isn't just resume speak but an actual description of the chaos. She'd been diligent about practicing grounding techniques after a panic attack at work left her so shaken she'd had to leave mid-meeting, sit in her car for forty minutes trying to breathe, genuinely convinced she was having a heart attack despite being thirty-two years old with no cardiac history.

The techniques helped. Actually helped, not in a placebo way but in a real "I can interrupt this spiral before it takes me all the way down" way. When panic started rising, she could use box breathing. Could anchor herself with the 5-4-3-2-1 sensory exercise. Could bring herself back from the edge.

But even on days when she didn't panic, when she successfully managed her anxiety and made it through without needing to escape anywhere, she felt perpetually on edge. Exhausted. Irritable. Snapping at her partner over nothing. Crying in her car on the drive home for reasons she couldn't articulate.

Surviving, but nowhere close to thriving.

When we mapped out her daily routine—actually wrote it down hour by hour, which she resisted because "it's not that complicated"—a pattern emerged immediately. She worked late most nights, sometimes until eight or nine, fueled by a steady drip of coffee and whatever she could grab quickly. Breakfast was coffee and maybe a protein bar if she remembered. Lunch was whatever the vending machine had or a sandwich from the place on the corner that she'd eat at her desk while answering emails. Dinner was takeout or delivery, chosen based on how quickly it could arrive.

She prioritized sleep in theory. Knew she needed eight hours, had read all the articles about sleep hygiene and the importance of rest. But she consistently found herself scrolling through social media until one or two in the morning, her brain lit up by blue light and the particular poison of comparison anxiety—everyone else's curated highlights making her own life feel small and chaotic and behind.

Exercise meant the frantic sprint to catch the bus in the morning, her heart already racing from adrenaline before she even got to the office.

It wasn't that she didn't *want* to take better care of herself. She knew—intellectually, completely—that she should sleep more, eat real food, move her body in ways that didn't feel like punishment or frantic rushing. But she was overwhelmed. Stretched so thin she could see through herself. And honestly convinced she didn't have time for anything beyond crisis management.

Here's what becomes clear after you've worked with panic and anxiety for a while, after you've seen this pattern repeat across dozens of clients: regulation techniques are essential, they genuinely matter, but they're band-aids if you're not attending to the foundational needs of your body.

You cannot expect your nervous system to stay regulated when you're running it on four hours of sleep, nutritional chaos, chronic caffeine intake, and a constant drip-feed of cortisol. It's like expecting a car to run smoothly when you never change the oil, never rotate the tires, keep pushing it to redline, and then getting frustrated when the check-engine light comes on.

Sure, you might make it a few miles on determination. Might even make it a few years. But eventually the system fails. And then you're not just tired—you're completely dysregulated in a way that no amount of breathing techniques can compensate for.

We started small. Because the last thing Maya needed was to overhaul her entire life while already running on fumes. That's a recipe for failure, for adding one more thing to the impossible list and then feeling like a failure when you can't maintain it.

She committed to turning off her phone one hour before bed. That's it. Not meditating or journaling or doing a full nighttime routine. Not even reading something improving or educational. Just: phone off at eleven, do whatever felt good that didn't involve a screen. Some nights she read. Some nights she listened to music. Some nights she just lay there staring at the ceiling, bored out of her mind, her brain still wanting that dopamine hit of scrolling.

She started packing lunch the night before. Not elaborate meal prep, not Instagram-worthy bento boxes. Just: protein, vegetables, something she'd actually eat instead of grabbing whatever was fastest.

And instead of forcing herself into gym sessions she genuinely dreaded—the fluorescent lights, the crowded equipment, the feeling of being watched and judged—she started taking short walks during her lunch break. Fifteen minutes. Just around the block. Focusing on the physical sensation of her feet hitting pavement, the air against her skin, the sounds of the city around her.

None of this was dramatic. No one was going to write a transformation story about it. She didn't post before-and-after photos or start a wellness Instagram documenting her journey to optimal health. There were no dramatic breakthroughs, no single moment where everything clicked into place.

But six weeks in, Maya reported sleeping more soundly. Not perfectly—she still woke sometimes—but falling back asleep instead of lying there for hours. Feeling less reactive to the daily stressors that used to send her nervous system into overdrive. Having energy in the afternoons instead of hitting the 3 p.m. wall and desperately chugging more coffee just to make it through.

She still experienced anxiety. It didn't vanish. But she had more resources to work with it when it showed up. More capacity to use the regulation skills she'd learned instead of being so depleted that even pulling out a technique felt impossible.

The self-care industrial complex has made this concept almost meaningless, buried it under bubble baths and face masks and hashtag-self-care-sunday posts that treat it like indulgence. Like something you earn after you've worked hard enough, a reward for productivity.

But actual self-care—the kind that builds genuine resilience in your nervous system instead of just providing momentary relief—is much more boring and much more necessary than that.

Sleep. Real food that actually nourishes you. Movement that you enjoy enough to keep doing. Consistent routines that signal to your body, day after day, that the world is safe enough to rest in.

You already know this. Everyone knows you're supposed to sleep well and eat vegetables and move your body. This isn't revolutionary information. I'm not pretending to have discovered some secret wisdom that the rest of the wellness industry has overlooked.

But there's a difference—a crucial, often-overlooked difference—between knowing something intellectually and actually practicing it, especially when anxiety has you in survival mode where everything feels urgent and the idea of taking thirty minutes for a walk feels impossible when there's so much else demanding your attention.

And there's an even bigger difference between practicing these things as a means to an end—*I'll take care of my body so my anxiety goes away*—versus practicing them as a baseline way of living. *I'll take care of my body because it deserves care, regardless of whether my anxiety cooperates.*

That second version is harder. It requires letting go of the idea that you can earn your way out of discomfort through perfect adherence to the right techniques, that there's some formula where if you just do everything correctly, anxiety will finally leave you alone.

It means accepting that you might do everything "right"—sleep eight hours, eat well, move your body, practice your breathing—and still have days where panic shows up uninvited. Where your heart races for no reason you can identify. Where you wake up anxious and stay anxious despite your best efforts.

And that acceptance, paradoxically, is what makes everything else possible.

Living fully with awareness of your body isn't about creating a life so perfectly optimized that anxiety can't touch you. It's not about building high enough walls or developing strong enough skills that you finally become immune to discomfort.

It's about building a foundation strong enough to weather anxiety when it inevitably appears—and it will appear, because you're human and you have a nervous system designed to detect threats—and continuing to engage with your life anyway.

I think about this with my own presentation panic, the one I described at the start of this chapter. The skills I'd spent years learning and teaching didn't prevent the panic from showing up. My body still flooded with adrenaline, still interpreted the stakes of that presentation as life-or-death even though my rational mind knew better.

But what had changed—what all this integration work had built—was my relationship to the experience. I didn't need the panic to stop before I could function. Didn't need to wait until I felt calm before I could continue. The sensations could be there, loud and uncomfortable and genuinely distressing, and I could keep going.

Not because I'm particularly disciplined or because I've transcended normal human responses to fear. Because I'd practiced enough times, in enough different contexts, that my nervous system had finally learned: *this is not actually dangerous. This feels terrible, but it won't hurt you. You can survive this.*

That knowing—that deep, embodied sense of your own resilience—doesn't come from reading about it or understanding it intellectually. It comes from lived experience. From staying when everything in you wants to run. From noticing your heart race and not immediately catastrophizing. From building, slowly and incrementally, a track record of evidence that you can handle more than your anxiety wants you to believe.

The question isn't whether you'll still experience anxiety after doing all this work. You will. The question is: when it shows up, what becomes possible that wasn't before? What can you do now that fear used to forbid? What parts of your life can you reclaim?

And once you start reclaiming those parts—once you go to the party even with your heart racing, once you stay at the podium even when your hands shake, once you make the choice that scares you because it also calls to something deeper—everything starts to shift. Not all at once. Not in some dramatic transformation moment. But gradually, like a landscape coming into focus as the fog lifts, you start to see the shape of the life that was waiting on the other side of all that avoidance.

The life where your body is a source of information instead of a source of threat. Where you can feel afraid and keep moving. Where anxiety might still be a passenger, but it doesn't get to drive anymore.

That's what's waiting. Not perfection. Not the permanent absence of discomfort. Something better: the bone-deep certainty that you can handle whatever your nervous system throws at you, and the freedom that comes with that knowing.

Even with shaking hands and a racing heart, being *present* at your desk is a victory - a testament to the fact that you can navigate life even when anxiety isn't neatly resolved.

Also in the Series

Every book in Anxiety Reset stands on its own — read them in any order. If this one was useful, the library continues:

Anxiety for No Reason

Nighttime Anxiety

High-Functioning Anxiety

Anxiety Behind the Success

Anxiety in Public

Anticipatory Anxiety

Anxiety and the Overthinking Loop

Undiagnosed Anxiety

Anxiety and the Worry Habit